Ocean Stories

written & illustrated

BY OLIVIA LENTCHNER

ISBN 979-8-9856659-0-1 (paperback)

To my parents, who gave me the gift of my education,

and to all the amazing teachers and professors

who taught the wonders of the world around me.

TABLE OF CONTENTS

ACKNOWLEDGMENTS

THIS BOOK COULD not have been written without the beautiful stories of twelve phenomenal individuals. I would first like to thank my grandmother, Frances, and her husband, Jim, for agreeing to participate in this project as well as all the other featured contributors: Jude, Elliot, Meg, Aaron, Key Seok, Lesley, Johnny and my dear, dear friends, Sophie, Olivia, and Kathryn. Thank you for your time and for trusting me with your precious memories; I hope I did them justice.

I would also like to thank my family. Mom, Dad, Lillie, Andrew, and Maddie, the completion of this project would not be possible without your wonderful support and the amazing ways you each bring such light to my life. I love you all immensely!

A big thank you also goes out to Dr. Keiner. Thanks for not only agreeing to take this project on as my faculty advisor, but also helping me navigate the route toward its completion. Your constant support during my time as an undergrad at CCU allowed me to achieve all the goals I set out to accomplish. I thank you for this and all the meetings, emails, texts, and zoom calls over these past couple of years.

Likewise, I really appreciate Mrs. Phillips, my tenth-grade English teacher, and Jena, my new graphic design friend, for taking the time out of their busy schedules to look through my pieces and help me finalize my edits. The final product turned out even better because of your marvelous input. Thank you both for aiding me in my endeavors!

Lastly, I would like to recognize all the teachers, professors, and mentors that helped shape me into the person I am now. I was able to grow under your stewardship and learned so much from all that you had to offer. My parents always tell my siblings and I, "Even when everything else is gone, no one can take away your education," so I thank you for giving me the gift of knowledge.

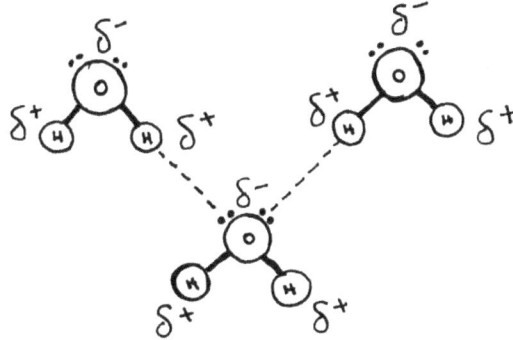

INTRODUCTION

As an aspiring marine scientist, I have learned about the miraculous properties of water that make it perfectly suited to sustain life. Water is awesome! It is a polar molecule with a high heat capacity and a solid form that is less dense than its liquid state. Furthermore, the polarity of H_2O gives it the ability to form hydrogen bonds by the attraction between like or other molecules. This quality itself accounts for amazing phenomena, such as adhesion and capillary action, explaining how water is transported from the roots, through the stem, and to the leaves of plants.

Putting science aside for a moment, in literature, the life-giving properties of H_2O are described in a different light. In artistic expression, water is a symbol of life, rebirth, and purification. It is viewed as a pure and cleansing element of nature with cool and calming connotations. I like to think that there is truth and beauty in both the scientific and artistic definitions of this natural property. In fact, I would say that they describe the same things in different ways and thus are not completely separate from one another.

The power of creative expression connects us back to nature. There is something profound and invigorating in this relationship. Moreover, I would call science the *language of creativity*. It is the literature that describes the art form of nature. Scientific education is of utmost importance because it allows one to enhance their perspective of the world by understanding its language. I like to tell people it is one thing to walk on a beach at sunset; it is another thing altogether to walk on the beach at sunset and know all the names of the shells along the shore, or the process of setting angle and reflected colors that make up the sunset.

In a book that my brother so graciously gifted me, called *Vesper Heights,* the author, Helen MacDonald, describes this same sensation in a much more eloquent manner. She explains:

> "For there's an immense intellectual pleasure involved in making identifications [...] the natural world becomes a more complicated and remarkable place, pulling intricate variety out of a background blur of nameless grey and green"

MacDonald describes this opportunity as "the joy of encountering something I already knew but had never seen before." It is through science the experience is elevated, and a new level of wonder is unveiled. It is important to instill these marvels in our youth and our communities, but the way science is communicated puts limits on the population to which the information is conveyed.

Much of our world is dependent upon water. Organisms rely on water for survival, the human body is roughly seventy percent water, and water covers most of our planet. However, even though the marine realm fabricates the majority of the biosphere, very little is actually known about it. In the scientific community, we continue to make progress in uncovering the mysteries of the ocean, but such discoveries are communicated in formal journal articles that are restricted to a certain audience. In such publications, flowy language is discouraged, and the passive voice is employed. In doing so, any personal connection to the project is stripped away entirely, while data and findings are correlated in numbers, graphs, and figures.

There is merit and validity to this process, and there is a beauty and art to graphs and numbers, for they are pictures and values that symbolize the connections of the world and its hidden complexities. Rather, I mention the pitfalls to highlight the inaccessibility of such works to the everyday individual. I had to go to college under a science program to learn to read and write scientific papers, and even if one can read such works, most journals require one to pay for viewing access of a given piece. I say all this not to bash the system fully, nor do I deny that there is a need for a standard, but this form of communication serves as a disadvantage in relating science to the general public.

I want to pursue a different avenue of scientific communication. One that can be related to people from all different walks of life and is based on our innate relationship with the creativity of nature, so that everyone can see how remarkable our world is. It is therefore my hope and dream to employ some sort of creative element in every research project I do. Whether that is making a children's book to go along with the study, interviewing the local fishermen, making all the graphs into art pieces and holding a gallery, etc. The possibilities are endless!

The goal of *Ocean Stories* is to juxtapose the fields of art and literature with the realm of science. In this manifestation of that aspiration, I ask a variety of individuals to recount a memory they have of the ocean. The scope of the memory or type of experience was not limited, but there was a surprising similarity between all the tales that, in many ways, acts as a reflection of people's connection to nature and its effect on the soul. I interviewed twelve willing participants ranging from ages eight to almost eighty, and despite the widely diverse array of backgrounds and personalities, there was a common depth in each of their relationships with the water. In addition to this quality, I noticed many of my orators expressed a longing to continue their beach-going adventures. This pattern was evident in the way many of them spoke of "family still going every year," or "trying to make it a normal place for us to retreat to." Several even mentioned retiring on the coast. Not only does a link with the ocean exist, but it also persists. There is a pull and an attraction, much like the very hydrogen bonds between water molecules and other particles or the ebb and flow of the tides.

This anthology is a collection of people's memories with the sea. Each memory is reproduced in the form of poetry, and preceding each poem is the individual's story that inspired it. The tales are taken directly from my interviews and are told in the words of my participants. As the reader embarks on this sea-going journey, I would encourage them to read the story before the poem. In this way, one has the opportunity to absorb the beautiful stories as they are and follow the inspiration behind the pieces.

People are shaped by their own life experiences; events make up one's individual journey but still connect them back to the biosphere. We are individuals, but we are also under one world and can be connected through our experiences with water. I hope that this collection of stories is able to relay this message.

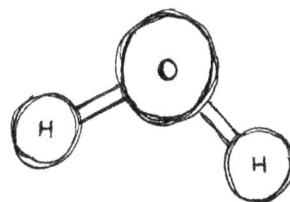

1

KATHRYN

MY FIRST EXPERIENCES with the ocean were when I was in the womb, which I use as a funny little reminder of the fact that I always loved the ocean. Since being born, I had the privilege of vacationing to a beach pretty much every year of my life. So, from early on, that one week on a Delaware beach with my family was the greatest week of my year, and I always looked forward to it.

Within my first year of life, we went to Ocean City, Maryland, but then every year after that, we went to Delaware. It has been a family tradition on my mom's side for several decades. It is silly that a family vacation to a touristy place was how I experienced marine science, but that was my exposure to that world. It just takes one encounter with something or someone to have a moment where you realize what is important to you.

I remember there was one year, I was no older than ten, and I thought I was so cool for writing poetry. We have to cross this bridge over the Chesapeake Bay to get to the beach, and I wrote this poem about the Chesapeake Bay and how blue it was. I remember another time sitting on the beach and writing a poem. I couldn't tell you what it was about; it was probably really bad! Talking about it feels silly, but I also think it's magnificent that something that was a wonder to me in childhood is still the same. As a child you are always bouncing about and full of energy, being at the beach and always wanting to be in the water. As I got older, I slowed down, not necessarily in a bad way. The cool part is that whether I'm bouncing around in the waves or being lazy laying out in the sand, I'm still taking in each moment and appreciating it on a broader scale.

I was also fortunate to vacation in Florida. Once again, in a very touristy spot, but amongst the tourism, there were opportunities to snorkel or visit a small local aquarium and learn about the marine life and, very vaguely, about the ecosystems in which they exist, and how that plays into the functions of our world and below the ocean.

On a deeper level, there was always that innate sense of wanting to always know more, to learn, to protect, and to teach other people about it too. Growing up, in school we started to learn about climate change. This is newer terminology and a newer crisis discipline that is becoming increasingly something that we cannot ignore. Despite all the increasing greenwashing and the failures that we still have in terms of reducing our carbon footprint, there are great initiatives that are out there, and more people becoming aware of the global climate crisis and ocean pollution. More people want to do something about it, even if it is not their career. They see the value in the ocean and the surrounding ecosystems, and they know that it is something worth saving.

I don't know the exact moment when I decided to pursue marine science, but it was definitely influenced by when I interacted with marine mammals or was immersed in the ocean or a body of water. In my public school system, every sixth grader spent a week at outdoor school at a nearby nature center. For a week we learned about the microecosystems there and explored the little creeks. I assume we learned about the Chesapeake Bay, but we got to see nature hands-on. The week itself was bad just because of me being an awkward sixth grader sharing a cabin with other girls I didn't really know or like, but I still look at the memory fondly and as a pivotal moment just because I remember being so fascinated. Even if the information was not particularly new and exciting, just being immersed in nature, being able to touch it and feel it and soak in all the information, was the best feeling in the world.

These interactions prompted my admiration for the ocean. When you love something, you want to take care of it. This was relevant even more so as an undergrad when I had started my degree. A lot of individuals, myself included, had only ever really thought about marine mammals as part of marine science and the marine biology side of things. Being a marine science student really broadened my perspective of what marine science meant because it's a more interdisciplinary study of the field. I even got an extra education in sustainability. This was another pivotal moment for me because I was able to see the interconnectedness of humanity and marine life and the environment in general, which is so awesome! There is no better way to describe how we really are connected to this earth and this world.

My education deepened my appreciation for the ocean. It is still this big, beautiful mystery, and for me, learning about it makes me want to learn even more and takes me back to the little child that I was. We learned about deep-sea exploration briefly in our studies, but the amazing things that exist thousands of feet below the surface of the ocean are something that makes you question life, and you have this existential moment when you learn about things like that, but in a good way. Just like when learning about deep space and space exploration, we want to learn more about the unknown and understand the world we exist in.

Sometimes I laugh at how mediocre my story sounds. I mean, I wish I grew up in a small seaside town living in a cottage collecting shells, but it's not that. It's not that glorious, but to me, it is still something special. My family still goes every year (when I was in college, I might have missed a year or two). That is something that we share as a family: memories of the ocean, spending time at the beach. We might not see each other often, but it's a way for us to come together and reminisce on our childhood, playing together in the sand or water, and wondering in amazement about it.

PERSONA OF MY DEAR FRIEND, THE OCEAN

I heard the ocean calling my name

Before I even knew what my name was.

The ebb and flow of a galaxy of deep

Mysteries beckoned tiny toes to

Explore the enticing pool of majesty.

The sensation was magnificent, and

I ventured further into the otherworldliness.

This oasis was steadfast and remained

By my side through many seasons of growth,

Always in the background of my thoughts.

That seaside in Delaware and the familiar

Journey across the Chesapeake.

I began to get to know her,

This persona of the sea, and the

Childlike bewilderment that she instilled in me.

I saw her presence everywhere I went.

She exists in the little creek beside the nature center.

I squat on the banks in quiet contemplation.

I let her idiosyncrasies fill up the space in my head.

A slight grin flashes across my face as a

Dazzling school of aquatic memories swims past.

She painted constellations of interconnectedness.

I was granted access to this art gallery

And gained insight into the intricate

Beauty of the world's greatest dot-to-dot.

The smaller details still baffle me,

But I am not alone in my eagerness

To learn more about them. I immerse

Myself in the silly clichés that tell me to

Follow my heart and lead life with passion.

It just takes one encounter with something,

Or someone, to have a moment

Where you realize what is important to you.

I realized that then, and I reflect on it now:

All those beautiful moments spent in her wake.

She is powerful, and she continues to call my name.

Elated, I plunge back into that universe

Beyond human belief, following the siren's call.

I will continue to seek the treasures of a hidden

Kingdom and surrender my wandering path

To whatever direction the current pulls me towards.

2

JOHNNY

I PROBABLY STARTED sailing with my dad when I was about seven or eight. Sailing's great. What makes sailing great, especially short-handed sailing (short-handed sailing is when you sail with just one or two people on a boat) is that there are so many things to focus on. You're thinking about how you've got your engine and you've got your sails. You've got to know the weather, the charts, navigation rules, how to trim the sails, different sail combinations, all the electronics on your boat, etc. It's just a ton of stuff. I mean, a fifty-foot boat with just one person on it, that's a lot of things to do at once, but that's what makes it interesting.

So, the story that I have about the sea is about picking up a boat that I had from Bermuda: a 1998 Swan 48. It was about a fifty-foot sailboat, and I named her Isabelle, after Isabelle Autissier (now that's somebody worth reading about! She's the real deal in sailing, and I was very impressed with what she was able to accomplish). I flew into Bermuda in April, about 2002, and met three guys who had brought the boat up from the Caribbean, one of whom I knew, and the other two who were just there helping out. When I got there, it was bad, stormy weather. The whole thing was a mess. I think it was actually the earliest recorded tropical storm in that area, and so we waited a day and then decided it wasn't going to get any better anytime soon, so we set off to Rhode Island. That was sort of where we got started.

The way we set it up is we had two teams. The guy I was with knew the boat incredibly well and was a very seasoned sailor. In fact, he and I were going to do the race two-handed from Newport to Bermuda, but I ended up not being able to do it for work reasons. The other guy was a very seasoned captain, and the fourth guy was not particularly seasoned at all. At one point we realized that he didn't know how to steer the boat at all, so that meant, okay, we're down to three people over five days... We tried to keep two people on deck, two people below resting, so we would do shifts. I think we were running three-hour shifts. Three hours on, three hours off, three hours on, three hours off, etc.

Anyways, not too long after we got out, things got a little bit choppy. The wind was blowing about thirty to thirty-five knots, which probably gusts a little bit higher. We had a little bit of a jib and a storm sail out. It was a storm trysail hooked up as a sort of a storm staysail, so not a lot of sail for a fifty-foot boat because, I mean, all you needed to do was hold up a napkin, and you go!

The seas were pretty big. They got pretty big pretty fast. Running peak to trough, they had to be a good fifteen to twenty feet, but just the top couple of feet were breaking, so they weren't really dangerous waves. What made it tricky is when you come off one of these waves you have to steer your way around so that you don't fly off the end of the wave and then drop ten feet, because that's like dropping your boat on concrete. It's a little trickier at night because you can't exactly see, but you can feel it. We weren't moving that fast because we were going upwind. It was a lot of wind, and the waves were coming at us, so it was really slow, plodding progress.

One of the problems, when you're coming up on deck, is there's always a risk you could end up going overboard. So, you lay these very flat lines on both sides of the deck and tie them down. You got a harness on, so anytime you come up top you clip in. That way, if you do go overboard, you're not instantly lost, because if you go overboard, there's probably a very low chance of getting back. You do this when the seas are rough or at night.

I remember one night in particular; we had a whole series of thunderstorms around us. There must have been three?... four?... five?... of them. It was kind of beautiful to see these thunderstorms in different areas, and you really realize how localized weather can be. We had to work our way around them. The problem with thunderstorms for a sailboat is wind sheer. If the wind's blowing forty to fifty miles per hour, and you've got the right sails up, and your boat can handle it, you're fine, but if suddenly it's coming from 180 degrees the opposite direction, that becomes problematic.

I remember one time we came flying off a wave, and even though I was still holding onto the ladder and hadn't actually gotten up on the deck, I almost got shot overboard! From there! There is a clip on the side of one of the lazarettes where you sit so that you can clip in as you're coming up the ladder. I was reaching to clip into that, but it happened so quickly. It was really amazing how you get thrown around! I remember going to the bathroom one time. I stepped into the bathroom and was standing there for a second, and we hit a monster of a wave. We dropped off and hit the trough, and I hit my head against the mirror so hard that I looked at myself in the mirror and was like, *wow, I'm still conscious, ha!* I was really surprised because it was a real headbanger.

In a similar vein, a little interesting thing happened another night. I was actually on the wheel, and the other guy was standing in front of me. All of the sudden, he's just cursing. I was confused; I mean, *what the hell could be wrong all of a sudden in the middle of the ocean?* So, I said, "What's wrong?" It turns out, a flying fish hit him in the face, and because it was the middle of the night, he never saw it coming! Suddenly he's standing there and then *BANG*, he gets whacked in the head by a flying fish. That must've been a pretty miserable experience. He fired up a cigarette immediately thereafter.

There is a good bit of unpredictability and adjustment. When you go up front to change the sails, you're in the head of the boat just getting tossed around and doused with buckets of seawater all the time. The good news was I had this great offshore gear and, I swear to God, even though it was cold, and there was water everywhere all the time, I was super comfortable, which shocked me! I was warm and dry and happy and comfortable. It really worked well, so thank God for that one!

It's also hard to make any food, but fortunately, the guy I knew was very good and managed to do some cooking in spite of the fact that we were pounding and pounding and pounding. That's critical because the way people really screw up these things is they get cold, they're not fed, they're not thinking that clearly, they get hypothermic. I had that happen to my cousin when he and I were out one time. Things start to unravel really fast, and it can get pretty bad. You need to keep eating and drinking, and you need to stay warm and dry because it's cold, and it's blowing like crazy, so the wind chill is incredibly low. The wind and the water will just drench you, and that combination is a killer. If not a killer, it certainly will dull the senses at a time when you really don't want them dulled.

Having said all that, I was very comfortable throughout the whole experience, except for when I rapped my head into the mirror. That was not so comfortable. For whatever reason, and it's not because I'm particularly courageous or anything, there was just a comfort level associated with being with the sea and with sailboats, knowing how to sail, being in charge, and the control factor there. Even though there was not another boat in sight for four days – we were out in the middle of the Atlantic, I mean, there was nothing – it's just much more comfortable. I remember at one point looking at the boat, and it's a fifty-foot boat that weighs 29,000 pounds, and looking at the seas and saying, "You know what... This isn't really any bigger than a kayak." I mean, that's how you feel about it when you're in the middle of the ocean. I suppose I should have been a little bit uptight, but I really wasn't. Again, it's not a particularly courageous thing, it's just sort of things that you're comfortable with and things that you're not.

In the whole trip, we did finally run into one, single ship. It was so stormy that we figured because the boat was pretty big, they might never see us. They could just *BOOM*, run over us, and the only time they would know that anything had happened is when they painted the hull! Anyways, contacting those guys by radio was pretty important to make sure we didn't somehow inadvertently get run over.

Then as we got close to the United States, we got through the tropical storm and then got hit with a Northeaster, which was worse than the tropical storm because it ran into the Gulf Stream. The Gulf Stream's running north at four knots, and the Nor'easter's coming down at thirty-five knots plus, and it turns the waves from these pretty manageable waves that we had into these blocks. We were trying to figure out when exactly we were going to get in the Stream, and I remember distinctly, I was down below sleeping, and all of a sudden, man, it was just like *BA-DA-BA-DA-DA!* It was much rougher, and we were just getting banged around! It was pretty violent. I was like, *well, I'm not going to sleep through this*, so I went up top. We were in the Stream, and there was no doubt about it. The shape of the waves had changed completely. It's not that the waves were bigger, they were just shaped very differently, and there was more breaking, which made it more difficult.

We got through the Gulf Stream, and then everything sort of calmed down a bit. One morning, I came up on deck, and we were surrounded by like a hundred dolphins. Porpoises or dolphins, I couldn't really tell if they were one or the other. They stayed with us for a long time. I went up into the bow and hung out up there for a bit, and they were all around the boat and just jumping everywhere. It was great! They really sort of played with the boat. You hear about people having this sort of experience, but I never had it myself, so that was pretty neat as well.

We got into Rhode Island at night and tied up. It took maybe five days to make the whole trip, which is pretty long. We were actually able to put up a spinnaker and sail in nice and easy. We were pretty beat up by the time we arrived. When we got off the boat, it was really tough. After you've been on a boat that's been moving so aggressively for so long, when you get off on the dock it's really hard to walk. I mean, you've been up and down twenty feet for the last four and a half days; we got off, and it was like nothing stopped moving.

So, what did we do? We went straight to the nearest bar where there were a bunch of people waiting for us. We were late getting there, so these people were a little worried because they knew the weather had been bad and that we were behind, so we finally let everybody know when we got within radio contact. We headed there, and we ate and drank as much as possible. And slowly, I mean I can't remember how long it took, but it was definitely one to three hours before the floor stopped moving because we spent so much time just getting bounced around, and now, we were on a stable platform. It was weird.

THREE-HOUR SHIFTS

The seas roar in a series of frothy blocks as we hit the Gulf Stream,

And in my head rings the clamor of pounding waves.

It raps the sides of my consciousness in violent spurts,

Aggressive and abrupt.

I shall not escape to my dreams tonight

As the grim tempest clashes with the plodding surface current.

Buckets of seawater douse us daily,

And the wind blows in billowing gusts that whip across the face,

Chilling the inner sanctum of sanity with a potency that can dull the senses.

An organized cacophony of orchestral thunderstorms

Electrifies the dark sky.

So as to escape the clutches of the foreboding wind sheer,

We worm our way through the turbulent troughs,

Amazed by such a spectacle and accompanied by

The harmonious pairing of light and sound.

As we journey past the raging waters,

A sole isle lost in the incomprehensible volume of the sea,

Hundreds of dorsal fins, wavelike in appearance and movement,

Emerge as sleek crests. A chorus of wandering shadows

Surging through the adjacent waters.

The porpoises' propensity for uninhibited merriment

Laps the sides of the vessel in playful effervescence.

Struck by these marvels, but our destination in mind,

We push on,

Navigating through the pleasures and treacheries of an ultramaritime dimension

Where man does not belong,

But the sailor longs to be.

The tides continue to churn,

And sometime after the fifth sunrise of our sojourn,

The once distant horizon of our destination is now within reach.

I groggily exit the seafaring domicile,

Still swaying to the palpitating rhythm of perpetual waves.

Upon arrival, we indulge in the festivities granted

Through the commodities of food and drink,

Tired from our quest and hungry for camaraderie.

Hours pass before the room stops spinning.

My body readjusts to the reality of my position as a lifeform on land,

As though my time away was but an underwater dream,

But my thoughts will forever roll

With the push and pull of the tantalizing current

That beckons me seaward

To sail another day.

Sailing is an artform,

A juxtaposition of knowledge in adverse domains:

The mechanical and the natural.

There are so many different things to focus on,

But I find comfort in how these conflicting elements come together

And derive some semblance of control in the ubiquity of it all.

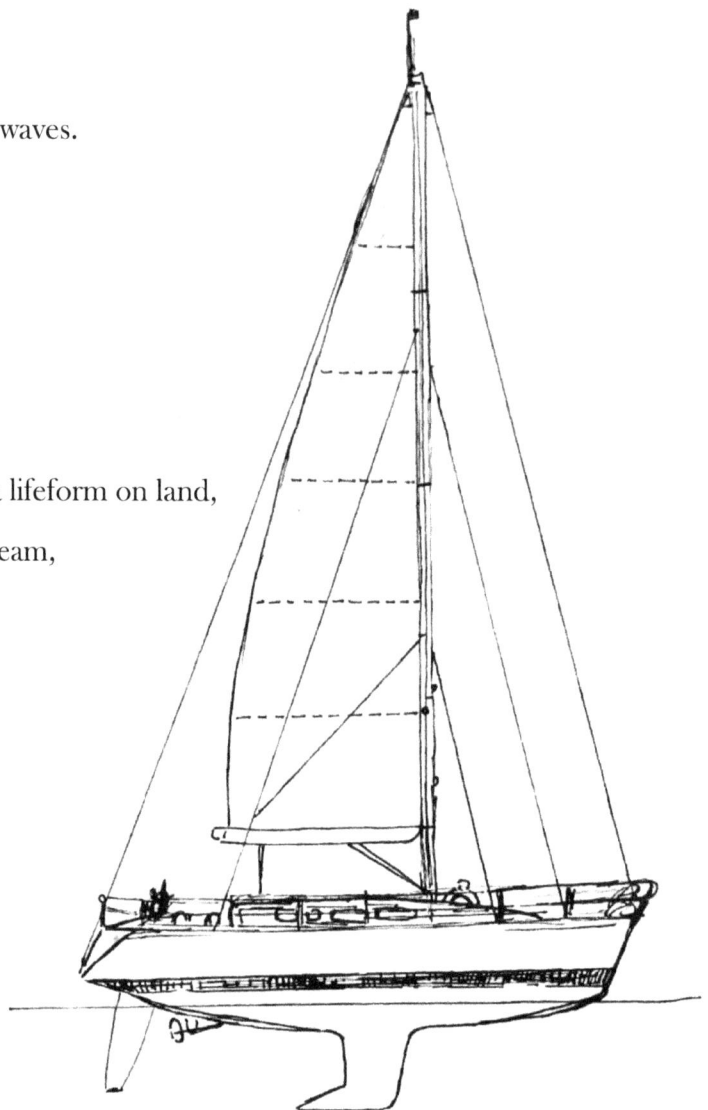

3

JUDE

I HAVE A LOT of ocean memories; almost all of them are in Sanibel, like finding sea stars or sand coins, sand dollars. We usually go every two years, but sometimes every year. We also go to national parks on our summer breaks. I like Yellowstone or the Grand Canyon. My favorite part about the Grand Canyon is that it's so long and wide. In Yellowstone, there's so much mountains and grass and flowers and trees.

When we're in Sanibel, I like to make sandcastles mostly. The biggest one I made was with my mom and my brother. Well... that was the *widest* one. The *biggest* one was just with my brother. We go to sand bars and stuff, and that's where we find sea stars and sand dollars. You have to scoop them. You feel them with your feet, and then you can go underwater and scoop them up. They're alive.

One night there was really clear water. We saw shells and sand, and it was shallow. Me, my brother, and my mom went into the ocean for a swim, and we saw a baby sea turtle swimming going into the ocean. We were in the ocean. It wasn't deep in the ocean. The turtle just hatched, and it went into the ocean, and that was at Sanibel Island.

We were playing volleyball, and like every day one year for about a week, we saw a snake slither by the volleyball thing. Oh yeah, and we saw there's a little pond where there's an alligator in it right by the condos. And also, by the pool, there was an iguana who went by. He came out of the bushes, and he was like, "hi."

Also, we sometimes got up early and did a beach walk, saw the sunrise, and picked up shells. We are walking and then coming back to our condo. It's orange, pink, and red. Those are the main colors that I've seen, oh yeah, green too! It was near the sun, and they were all mixing, the colors were, a little bit like painting. And we saw dolphins in the early morning. We also saw one up close. On a night there was a sand bar, we were near the sand bar, and we saw dolphins just going so close to us and swimming by. They were just swimming.

There was also a sandstorm once. We didn't go out in it because it was a storm. Well, in the morning we did go boogie boarding at first, but then my dad said, "Those are really big waves," and he wanted us to get out of it. My dad went back to the condo, and my mom was working at the condo, and my dad left me with my brother, and my other brother, and me. A storm came in, and sand started blowing. When we first realized it, me and my brother, we noticed that it was starting to get windy. He felt a raindrop, and we saw the clouds, and my other brother was like, "Nah, it's just passing by." It started blowing everywhere, and it got worse and worse, and sand got in my eyes all the way to dinner! It didn't hurt when it hit me, it just made me close my eyes a lot, and the waves were like crazy! They were huge! They were great for boogie boarding.

Oh yeah, one more thing: once we were at a really far sand bar from the beach, and there were huge waves, and I brought a boogie board. It was me, my mom, and my dad. Neither of my brothers came. Well... they did come... and then me and my brothers went back in, and then I was wondering where my mom and my dad were, and then I spotted them way out. So, I got a boogie board and went out there to the sand bar and there were big waves, but I had a boogie board, and it was really fun!

THE SUN RISES ON SANIBEL

I once met a sea turtle on Sanibel Island,

And it was here that I bravely encountered

A plethora of other audacious ventures

And mysterious creatures.

I once traversed the daunting coastline

In the midst of a raging sandstorm,

A formidable foe, to say the least,

But I won the battle, eyes closed!

I faced ferocious waters and ginormous waves

With the aid of my trusty boogie board,

To reach the refuge of distant, sandy isles

Speckled with sea stars and sand coins.

Upon such bars of sand existed planets

Of exploration. Once the water was

Really clear, and I witnessed the shelly

Terrain of the ocean's shallows.

I also met a snake who was into volleyball.

He made it a goal to hit the court

At least once a day in order to

Stay in good shape.

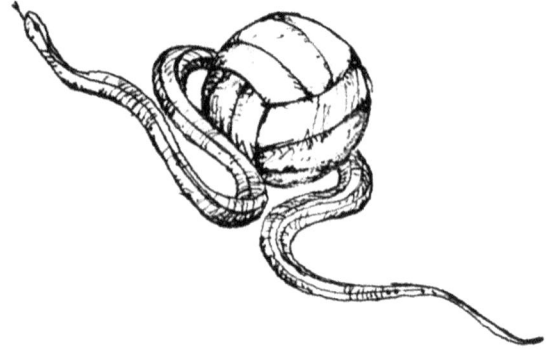

On a separate occasion, I met an iguana,

Who was just chilling by the pool,

As well as an alligator,

Who was interested in condo real estate.

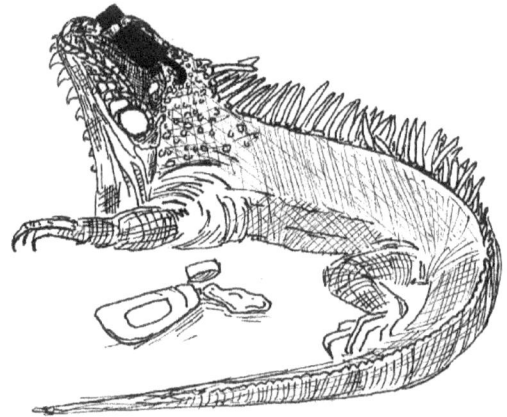

Being a building connoisseur myself –

An attraction mainly centered around

Wide or big sandcastle construction –

We had a mutual respect for one another.

I have a lot of ocean memories.

My many awe-inspiring escapades

Come in a variety of hues and shades,

Each one special and unique.

The individual oranges, pinks, reds, and

Sometimes even greens, mix together,

Like painting, to make something spectacular,

Resembling the sunrise of an early beach walk.

I will continue to seek the meandering boulevards

Where adventure awaits around every corner

And see the local color of a summery, exciting life,

Such as my time on Sanibel Island.

4

FRANCES

WE WOULD GO to the beach every summer when I was growing up. I had three great aunts, and one of my aunts had ownership of a two-story guesthouse in Myrtle Beach, South Carolina called The Anchorage. Most of the guesthouses at the beach were like this during this period of time, but today I think most of the coastline has been replaced by big, tall hotels. At the time, there was one large hotel close to town, and there was another huge hotel down at the opposite end of the beach away from town. That was one of the first hotels when the beach started to develop, probably long before I started to go there.

I started going to the beach more frequently when I was in the first grade because my family moved from Pennsylvania to Winston-Salem, North Carolina for my daddy's new job at Reynold's Tobacco Company. We lived in North Carolina in Winston-Salem until I went to college, and my family would go to the beach to The Anchorage as long as my aunt and my great aunt were there. There were several years that we stayed most of the summer because my mother was helping my aunt over at The Anchorage, but after that, we went maybe once or twice over the summer for maybe a week or two.

My mother was a schoolteacher, and that first summer we moved to Winston-Salem, there was time before Daddy started his new job, so my parents rented a house across the street from The Anchorage, and we spent the whole summer there. It was not nearly as large of a guesthouse as The Anchorage was; it was more like an older home that was turned into a guesthouse. There were about four to five bedrooms upstairs and maybe two to three downstairs. The Anchorage was always full all summer long. That summer, if The Anchorage was already full, my aunts would book guests a room and send them across the street to Mother and Daddy. In this way, people would come there if they had no place to stay, and so we spent that summer across from The Anchorage taking in guests. That was fun because I was down there for the whole summer.

I learned to swim in the ocean, even before I went to camp. When I went to camp in the mountains, I could swim just fine because I had learned in the ocean. I would always go horizontally, parallel to the shore, when I was swimming. I also just loved looking for shells. We would walk a lot on the beach, pick up those shells, and put them in a pail. At one point, I had a whole collection that I had gathered off the beach. Being on the beach was the highlight. That was what I enjoyed doing, and that was the most fun. We went twice a day. In the morning, we would come in, have lunch, and come back around two o'clock in the afternoon. We tried to stay out of the sun right in the middle of the day because that was the hottest time. I was as brown as a berry by the time the summer was over from the sun at the beach. I never sunburned, but my skin got tanned.

There was a big center in the middle of town in Myrtle Beach where they had a Ferris wheel, and a merry-go-round, and an amusement park. We would go up there just about every night, not when I was there for the whole summer, but whenever we would go for just a week or so, we would go every night there and enjoy the fun at the amusement park. Of course, there were always a lot of people there too.

The beach was just the highlight of people's summer in South Carolina, and they usually came once or twice during the summertime. There were interesting people that came to The Anchorage, all the way from grandparents down to children. During their stay, usually a group of people wanted to go crabbing while they were there at the beach. Several people went off on their own to go fishing, but The Anchorage would offer to take people out crabbing. Crabbing was always fun. One of my great aunts would organize a trip that went down the road from Myrtle Beach in one of the areas where there weren't a lot of people and hotels. We went out in the morning at low tide until early afternoon. There was a lot of marsh and open area out there, and you could go to the edge of that. We would go out to a place where you could get real close to the water. To crab, you have a long, long heavy string, and you would tie a fish head on it. Ahead of time, the staff would go and buy the fish heads that were left over from the people that sold fish. The fishermen would cut the heads off, and The Anchorage staff would go pick up those fish heads and kept them cold until we left. Then later, we would tie them onto the end of the string. I would help people tie it, and I thought that was such a good job. I got pretty adept at tying the fish heads during those times, that was fun. I liked to put the fish head on the line. After tying the fish head on the end of the string, you would throw the line out in the water. There was also a pier, and you could walk out on it and throw the fish head over that too. You would wait until you felt a little nibble pulling on the end of that line, and then you would very, very slowly gradually pull it in to where you could see it. Then you would take the net and quickly scoop the crab up. We got home a little after lunchtime, and we would get to eat in the kitchen there at The Anchorage. At another time, they cooked the crabs in the kitchen for the guests.

They had a dining room at The Anchorage where guests ate breakfast, lunch, and dinner. There were several cooks that worked there full time. In fact, some of them came down with one of my aunts who lived in Greeneville and worked at the YMCA. Also, my aunt who lived in Burlington and taught school knew some cooks there and would bring them down in the summer, so we would have about three to four cooks in the kitchen, and they would serve three meals a day to the guests, except on Sundays. On Sunday, they only served 'til lunchtime. Nothing was served at night, and that gave the people that worked in the kitchen some time off. They had a small house next to the hotel that they stayed in. Most of them didn't have a car, so the staff sometimes took them to see things when they were off work. It was always very good food. I don't know how they managed three meals a day! I liked to go over and watch them work on their hair. It was just fascinating the way they braided and did such a good job.

I had a mischievous friend, and I got myself into some trouble. Mary Ann Sanders was her name. I also had a friend named Mary Ann Hart, but at that time, Mary Ann Sanders and I were in the same room in the second grade, and we both were taking ballet lessons at the same time. Her mother took me home from school on the days we had dance lessons, and she would take me to the dance lessons because my mother was teaching. So, Mary Ann Sanders and I were really good friends. We were in the second grade probably, and Mary Ann's family had heard about The Anchorage and thought they would like to go for a week the next summer. That was one of the summers Mother worked there and helped my aunts out, so they called up, and Mary Ann Sanders and her family with her little sister came down to the beach.

She was extremely smart, Mary Ann Sanders, and I think she was sort of ahead of her time trying to do stuff. She discovered we could walk up the steps that led to the dining room, and then there was another little group of rooms up there that went out toward the road, and this was way up on the second floor. There was a rail and banister that went along there for the guests as they walked along to their hotel room. Well, Mary Ann Sanders had the idea that if we could climb up on that banister, we could climb on up to the roof on the second floor. She got it in her head that she would try to get up on the roof, and she encouraged me to come along, and I went right along with her. This roof came over the porch. She started getting up on that roof, and the ledge came down pretty low, but you had to put your leg way up to boost yourself onto the roof. Anyway, she hopped right up there and encouraged me to come on up there, and I thought, well... I had better do it... I should be able to do what she did... I *did* manage to get up on the roof, but I tell you what, I was trembling! We stood up on the roof because her mother, father, and little sister were walking along down there, and we were waving to them and were so proud and wanted them to see what we were doing. When her mother and father saw us, they said, "GET OFF THAT ROOF AND COME RIGHT DOWN!" I really didn't get into trouble, but she did. Her mother and father took her, packed their bags, and went to Winston-Salem that afternoon. They were there no longer. They took her away from the beach and went back home. Mother realized how she was and knew that never in the world I would do something like that. I was scared to death!

SUMMERS AT THE ANCHORAGE

Take me back to the 1950's along the Southern shore.

On the nostalgic coast of Myrtle Beach, South Carolina, my family was sheltered and cared for under the guesthouse roof that I dared to climb onto once with Mary Ann.

We got into so much trouble – her more so than I – but maybe it was worth it.

Southern hospitality nourished the welcoming atmosphere of The Anchorage, my home away from home.

It seeped from every corner of the two-story guesthouse and swirled along the open roads with the sea breeze.

An invitation to wade in the cool, crisp mornings and collect shells on the beach before being called in for lunchtime.

The hotel, an anchor in my memory, narrated by the many adventures schemed within its walls.

I enjoyed exploring the dining room amongst the culinary commotion or walking along the shoreline that ran parallel to the waters I learned to swim in.

My favorite activities that this homestead housed were my aunt's crabbing extravaganzas.

I became quite adept at tying the fish heads to the line; it is hard work, but the labor is not in vain.

There is a trick, you see, you must adhere to the slow rhythm of gradually pulling in the line after a bite before quickly swooping your net around to snatch up the crab in the blink of an eye.

Vignettes such as these line the bulwarks of my youth.

I earned the delightful pleasure of the ocean's company and got to know a place, and its people, and its intricacies.

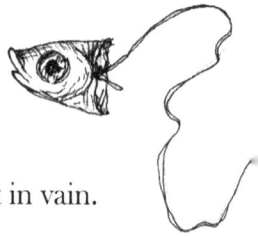

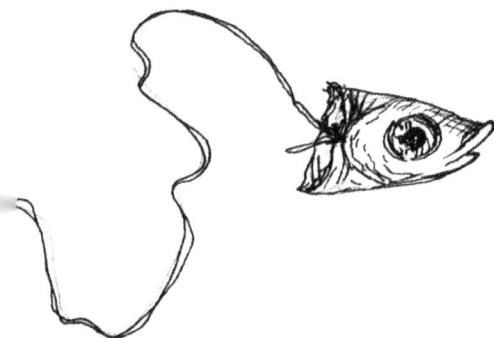

Take me back to those Southern, summer days filled to the brim with memories that will last a lifetime, even as everything else begins to fade.

Although my time there is now worlds away, the childlike sense of wonder is something that I maintain, moored upon the wharf of recollection.

Maybe my thoughts will never return to the simple ponderings of my former self, bestrewn with innocent questions such as:

"I wonder if we are going to ride the merry-go-round after supper tonight?"

but I continue to exude the same blithe spirit of the sweet child molded by the profound summers at The Anchorage.

I think back to the first-grader that I was, who, as brown as a berry, and clad in her favorite swimsuit, places shells in a pail with a big, toothy grin across her face.

I smiled then, and I smile now, simply at how wonderful it all is, the wonder of a place.

5

JIM

WHEN I WAS ABOUT eight, my mother; half-brother, who was six years younger than me; half-sister who was two and a half years younger than my half-brother; and I took a trip across the Pacific Ocean. We sailed from San Francisco to Japan and then down to Okinawa. My stepfather was in the Army, and he was already in Okinawa for about six months as the housing officer for the Ryukyu Command, which was the Army part of the station over there. The Korean War was going on, and that was why they were there, but the families were allowed to come, and they had a number of subdivisions for the families that were coming over.

In order to travel, children had to be over six months old. I don't really know why, but I assume it has to do with immunization records. Back then, as a child, I had a shot record, and you had to get all these shots to go overseas. I don't have the record anymore, but you had to have shots for a lot of things because of going to that part of the world. Anyway, we couldn't travel until my sister, Priscilla, was six months old. She was born while my stepfather was overseas.

We first flew from Baltimore to D.C. and then to Chicago, to Salt Lake City, and then on to San Francisco. When we were leaving, my mother had a list. You could take stuff, and you take certain furniture, but you could not get an automatic washing machine serviced over there, and there was no television on Okinawa. We had my parents' first television. It had little doors on the front of it, and the console pales in comparison to today's standards. My mother gave it to my grandmother before we left, but when we came back, my mother didn't have the heart to take it back from her.

As we were getting ready to go, my mother went and bought a wringer washer. On the day we moved, she had two moving vans, and they backed them up so that they could be both loaded from the center. They would bring the stuff out, and my mother just stood out in the street and would tell them which moving van to put the furniture in. Some went to storage, some were going overseas, but not a whole lot really went overseas. The wringer washer still had not been delivered, but on the day they were loading the vans a delivery man came up and saw the moving van and said, "Oh, this must be a mistake." My mother said "No, just put it in that moving van," and she stood there until the entire house was empty.

We moved over to my grandmother's, she lived close to the edge of Baltimore City about five miles away. I had started school, and then I had changed schools when we moved to my grandmother's. After a few weeks, we flew in a two-engine plane down to Washington D.C. I had never flown before, and neither had my mother, and we had all these bags that she needed to take on the plane because it was a long trip with a two-and-a-half-year-old and a six-month-old. When we got to the airport, they said that the load was too big and that we couldn't take it on the plane, so my mother went and got a handful of quarters and some shopping bags somewhere in the airport and unpacked everything right on the seats in the passenger area and then repacked it. She gave me a watch box and said, "Anything you can fit in here, you can take," because everything was going to the other children.

Anyway, we got on the plane, and we were sitting over the wing, and I had the window seat. We took off, and the engine on that side of the plane caught on fire. I mean, I was absolutely mesmerized. The flames were just shooting out of the back. It was like something out of a movie. It's not a long distance, Baltimore to Washington, and it was probably not much more than a fifty-mile flight. We were already up in the air, so they shut the engines off because we were probably almost halfway there. By the time you turn around and go back to Baltimore, we would have arrived at our destination already.

We flew down to D.C., repacked our luggage, and then got on a four-engine plane to fly up to Chicago. My mother bought three seats and was just going to hold Priscilla. They said the plane was almost full, but just before takeoff, they came around and said there was an empty seat up front. So, they took me up front and put me between two men. My mother came up at one point with Priscilla to see where I was sitting. As a child, I liked to talk to people, and I would ask them a lot of questions. I remember my mother's parting comment to the two men sitting on either side was, "If he talks to you, just slap him."

We got to Chicago, and it was a beautiful day. It was clear, and you could see the whole city. I was practically in the lap of the man next to me with the window seat, until finally he just gave me the seat. We arrived in San Francisco after stopping in Salt Lake City to refuel. I was sound asleep. We had to take an Army bus out to wherever we were staying. We were there for about two weeks waiting for the port call. They had a school for the children, so they sent me off to school. It was really more like a giant babysitting class. It was so crowded, they had to put two children at each desk, and we had to share a book. It was just glorified babysitting; I don't think anyone learned anything. I went to school there until it was time to get on the boat.

The boat was called the *S.S. Fultan.* It was a Navy ship. In World War II it had been a military ship, and after the war, they had refurbished it and put it back to a passenger ship. It was a nice ship as I remember, but by today's standard, it was probably pretty bare bones. There were two thousand women and children on the ship going to Okinawa. There were also men aboard the ship. The fantail of the boat was blocked off, so you couldn't go down the steps or anything, but you would see the men out there on the fantail because that was the only access they had to the outside. They were traveling to the same destination, but they were not allowed to mix with the women and children. They would wave sometimes. The passengers weren't allowed to go down there, and they weren't allowed to come up.

I had never been on a boat, and neither had my mother. They hollered "cast off!" and we got so seasick. I think part of the problem was never being on a ship before, but also, that late in the year, when we were about halfway across, there had been a typhoon there over toward Japan, and it got much rougher. There were certain expectations that you had to keep the room a certain way, and there were a couple of women who worked there that checked things out. You weren't allowed to have food in the rooms, but my mother kept crackers to help with seasickness. They wrote her up because she had a pack of crackers, but my mother had a terrible temper, and she gave the women hell. Absolute hell. And they never said anything again.

We had a cabin with a porthole; it had a fold-out bed from the wall and a set of bunk beds. They put a crib in there, but my mother had them take it out because there wasn't enough room. She slept in the fold-out with Priscilla across from her in the one bed, and then I slept on the top bunk with Charles. I slept at one end, and he slept at the other. I think he wet the bed every night. We also had a bath with a bathtub and no shower. There was another room next to ours that adjoined to the bathroom, but I don't believe it was occupied because, even though we shared a bathroom, the door that connected it to the other room never opened. My mother would make me give a bath to each child every morning, and my biggest fear was always that someone would walk into our bathroom while I was bathing the children.

I'm not quite sure how all the ranks worked, but my stepfather was a major when he left and promoted to lieutenant colonel while we were on our way over. After he was promoted, they told my mother that they were going to move us to better accommodations. The next step up was a bigger cabin and private bathroom. We did not end up moving, however, because my mother said she was settled there for the rest of the trip.

There was a place on the ship where they would play cartoons for hours every day, probably to entertain the children. Once, I was talking to another child around my age, and he showed me where his family was staying. There were bunk beds all the way around the room and no windows. There were probably nine to twelve beds, and I think three families shared a room. They shared a bathroom which I think was down the hall.

I wandered around some; I was a little more adventurous than some of the other children. I remember going onto one of the higher decks, and there was a gate there that was open. It led to the wheelhouse. I walked down, and there's all these people who worked on the boat. I still remember some sailors sitting in the ship, and one of the officers came over and asked, "How did you get in? You're not supposed to be down here." I told him the gate was open, and I walked on down, to which he said, "Show me." So I led him up to the end of the wheelhouse, and there it was, the gate, still unlatched. He was very polite about it, told me why I really wasn't supposed to be down here, then closed the gate, and latched it. He seemed to be more intrigued about how I had got there. I wasn't a bad child. I was just curious. I would go all over the ship.

We were at sea for two weeks over to Japan. When we got to Japan, we had to stay on the boat for two days. They told everybody on the port side to keep the curtains drawn, which is like waving a red flag to every child on the ship. Because the Korean War was going on, they opened up some service doors that were down on the side of the ship to load the bodies. They put out a canopy and brought out some soldiers, I think it was three on each side holding rifles as kind of a ceremony. For about two days they loaded the coffins because once the ship got to Okinawa, it was then going back to the states.

The day we pulled into Okinawa, my stepfather came up in a car with a driver and little flags in the front. A lot of the families rode in school buses, but he was given a car. I woke up in the morning, and you could see Mount Fuji from the boat. It parked, and we got off. There were no customs or anything.

I remember going to the beach once during our time overseas. There was a resort up at one end of the island, and the southern two-thirds of the island were tropical. We were bordered on the west side by the South China Sea. It was probably around early December. There was hardly anyone else out there. The water was not the color of the water here. It was kind of yellowish. I remember I would just wander around, and the waves would come up and bang against the beach. I found a boat down there, and it appeared abandoned, so I decided it was mine. I thought I could take the boat out in the ocean, but I couldn't get it moved. It wasn't a very big rowboat, but I also wasn't a very big child. It would not budge. Then this Okinawan boy appeared, and in a few minutes, his father was there. They lived there right along the beach; he was probably a fisherman. They were looking at me, and I think I asked them for help, but he just kept looking at me and looking at me and finally, I just left. It was their boat, and the little boy was probably concerned that I was trying to steal it.

I was eight when we left Baltimore and nine when we arrived in Okinawa. We were there for around a year and a half.

ABOARD THE SHIP TO OKINAWA

Little, eight-year-old me

Sailed on out to sea,

Eyes wide in wonder,

Shoulders weighed with responsibility.

My stepfather was in Okinawa to respond

Because the Korean War was going on.

He was a housing officer for the Ryukyu Command,

So my family went to meet him across the Pacific dawn.

Upon the waters the boat would rock,

So my mother kept crackers in stock.

A recent typhoon had the sea astir,

And seasickness gripped us with quite the shock.

We were at sea for two whole weeks.

I would wander around the boat stealing peeks

Of a new lifestyle unfamiliar to me,

The inner workings of a nautical feat.

I would wave to the men on the fantail

And venture farther beyond the rail

That led down to the secretive wheelhouse

Full of the workers that made the ship sail.

On one expedition, that I am aware,

A sailor told me I shouldn't be there,

But he seemed more intrigued with how I got in,

No easy task for a small child to bear.

Once in Japan, they said to keep the curtains closed,

But I was like a moth to a flame exposed,

So I parted the fabric to see the coffins loaded

In the bottom of the boat, escorted to repose.

When I was nine, we landed at last,

And at the dock in Okinawa, the anchor was cast.

Upon arrival I could see Mount Fuji,

An image etched from my distant past.

On the sands of an Okinawan beach, I explored

The tropical magnificence the islet bore.

I found a boat and claimed it as my own,

But soon found out it was already accounted for.

I spent a year and a half on this land across the sea,

Away from the earth I knew, and its familiarity.

Before this journey, I had never been on boat or plane,

But now that first experience is forever a part of me.

6

ELLIOT

ONE TIME I was at the ocean, and I was swimming with dolphins. I don't remember where it was... I think the Bahamas? It was pretty cool. The water felt really good, and also the dolphin literally got me in the air. It pushed me forward and got me flying!

DOLPHIN RIDE

It was cool,

Interacting with some ocean pals.

The duality of their existence,

Air and water,

I experienced both.

The sea, an avenue

Through which I was able to fly.

7

OLIVIA

WE'VE BEEN GOING to the beach at Ocean City, Maryland every year for my entire life. In fact, we still go! I used to be very scared of it. The waves were really not that intimidating, but I was afraid that I was going to die! I remember when I was very very little, I would sit by the waves, not where they would break, but where they come right up to the shore and the sand is wet. I used to build those little sandcastles on my knees. Because I was really afraid of it, I thought I could try making a contract with the ocean because, you know, that makes complete sense. I would write in the sand something like, *I will make the waves calmer so that Olivia can get in the water*, and then I would make a little *X* where I would sign my name. When the waves came up and washed away what I had written in the sand, that was the ocean signing my contract. By doing that, I was able to think, *okay, now I can get in the water!* I know logically that it did not work, but for a couple of years, I was like, *this is legitimate!* I would do that, and that was how I started getting in the ocean. I'm very happy I did it, no matter how ridiculous that is. Now I'm in every day, all day if I can!

Over the years, I think my view of the ocean has changed more than anything. I mean, like it is obviously this massive body of water, especially when you are at the beach looking out on the horizon, and there does not seem to be any end to it, but I remember as a kid just being completely blown away by how ginormous it was. When inevitably we went home and then came back the next summer, I would always forget how big it was, so it would blow my mind every year. I know that starting in middle school, as I got more into the ocean, I started to learn more about it, so every year I would go back to the beach with more knowledge. When I was young, the ocean would blow my mind because I didn't understand it, but now it started to amaze me because I did. I remember learning about horseshoe crabs and their range. I remember when I was younger and finally got into the water, if something bumped into my foot in the ocean I was like, *oh my god, that's a shark!* I was like four feet tall, so the water was even shallower than that, and so it was definitely not a shark, but at the time I thought, *this is where I die.* So then when I learned what horseshoe crabs were, and what they felt like, and where they lived, I was like, *that's just a horseshoe crab.* I remember when I learned how tides work. I didn't understand waves, and so they freaked me out because they were just so powerful and didn't make any sense to me, but then, when I learned about the tides, I was like, *the moon is doing that! That's bonkers!* It became really cool for a different reason, and I was able to maintain a fascination with the ocean. I think that it's cool that as I've gotten older, the fascination that started because I didn't understand the ocean has continued because now I do.

I think it is good that I grew up on a beach where the water was really murky because all I had to worry about was if something bumped into my foot, and of course, the waves. I've only been near super clear water very rarely, and one of the times was when I was kayaking while I was at whale camp in Canada. On this occasion, a jellyfish went past my kayak. It was really beautiful! I don't know what kind it was, but it was clear and had red arms, and it was just very gorgeous. At that point, I had gone to camp and had started studying marine science a bit more for myself personally, so I was like, *okay, I'm in a kayak. I'm fine,* but I know if I had seen that at a much younger age, I would have been amazed still but think, *that thing is gonna kill us! It's gonna flip the kayak!* The feeling surrounding it is the same, but it's just more informed. The ocean is one of those cool things that everyone is lacking a certain amount of knowledge about, so everything found out about it is something we get to all share in the excitement together.

I didn't become interested in the ocean because of my trips to the beach, but I became more interested in the ocean because of trips to the aquarium. I don't remember a time when I didn't know the aquarium existed, so I guess I started going when I was really young. When I started Kindergarten, my mom went back to work full-time, so the years before that, my mom would stay home with us. She and the mom next door would always be looking for things to do with us, and I'm sure that was one of our frequent ones.

One of my earliest memories at the aquarium was my eighth birthday. I knew what the aquarium was at that point and knew that it was where I wanted to be. When I would go to the aquarium, I got to see all the things I couldn't see when I went to the beach, and because of all the color and the energy of it, everything seemed all the more grand. I mean honestly, I would like to live under the ocean! It's all just so pretty! This opportunity to see the ocean in a way that I had never got to see it in person is what got me interested in it. The aquarium made the underwater world attainable for me. I mean, the odds of me going SCUBA diving in a coral reef early enough to know that that's what I wanted to do with my life was pretty low. I was not going to do that at like age eleven. Now the aquarium is where I volunteer over the summers as an exhibit guide. I wiggled my way in.

There was this one particular exhibit at my local aquarium with a three-legged green sea turtle named Calypso. They found her when she was very young, and she had an infection from an injury on her top left flipper, which resulted in the turtle version of hypothermia, or cold shock, so it had to be amputated. Because of related research, Calypso is part of the reason that scientists now know that turtles can survive with only three flippers. She is a big piece of this ginormous puzzle of understanding everything in the ocean. However, because she was part of discovering that, she had to stay at the aquarium for a long time because they didn't know yet if she could even survive. As a result, she became a permanent resident at my aquarium. I would make my family visit the aquarium as much as possible because I just wanted to see Calypso so bad. I attribute all my interest in the ocean and pursuit of marine science to Calypso. I have called Calypso my best friend for like ten years, which is an odd move, but she is my muse, and I love her!

It really bombs though, because she passed away a year ago while I was at school, and I didn't find out until that summer because my parents were like, "We can't tell her while she is at school." They knew I would lose my mind a little, and I kind of did when I eventually found out. It was the kid I babysit that actually broke the news to me. I was like, "We should go to the aquarium," and he was like, "Yeah, that big turtle's dead!" I said, "WHAT!" and then was like crying in their kitchen, but you know... I read her autopsy, and what I got from it was it was natural causes that would have happened anywhere. It was some sort of stroke or something is what I gathered. It all really stinks, but she is still part of a pretty big legacy.

A CONTRACT WITH THE SEA

I made a contract with the ocean

Based on mutual understanding.

I, being all too aware of my mortal standing,

Bargained for the ocean's power.

The foam-crested domain eating away at

The shore was all too strong and domineering,

So I took it upon myself to tell it so.

We struck up a deal, and the waves

Loaned me a deposit of courage.

I offered my sandcastle in return,

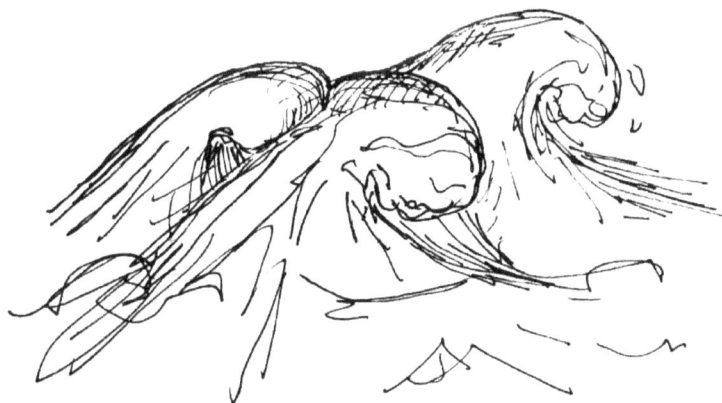

The barterer kindly accepted the tasty treat,

Devouring it in one or two bites.

I was simply relieved I did not share the same fate.

We were now bound, the sea and I,

And through a relationship founded on mutual respect,

A beautiful companionship began to take form.

Our eternal camaraderie

Ignited new perspective.

My small capacity of comprehension was

Challenged and expended by the sea.

Its surreptitious waves and ginormous breadth

Continuously blew my mind. I could not see

Past the horizon but was introduced to worlds that far

Exceeded such anthropocentric boundaries.

On the red tentacles of reverie,

I submitted to my fascination

And found myself a frequent guest to

The building the ocean called home.

The abode, bursting with grand aquatic splendor,

Summoned me. My heart decided to

Adhere to the beam of the persistent lighthouse.

I, a moth attracted to the flame.

I loved to walk the themed corridors

Of oceanic enchantment, that framed

Giant glass portals offering glimpses

Into a mystical kingdom of light and energy.

I remember the colors, colors that had never

Graced my eyes along the murkier waters of Ocean City.

They were brilliant and magnificent,

Summoning me toward this candy land of surrealism.

Two realities separated by a couple of inches

Of glass and an ocean of knowledge.

Then I saw her, the mesmerizing green

Of an island of miracles.

They called this stunning discovery,

Calypso, a captivating nymph

As lovely as Odysseus describes.

She represents an archipelago

Of scientific acumen and inquiry.

A big piece in this puzzle of understanding.

The weight of a legacy woven into

The molecular structure of her humble carapace.

This tripodal nekton encouraged me

To renew my contract with the sea.

I return to that beach in Maryland, as I have

Done every year, and write my conditions in the sand.

I then sign and allow the tide to wash away

The legal agreement, as this is its way of a signature.

The terms are acknowledged, and

I once again receive a deposit of courage

From my steadfast lender.

We will always be bound, the sea and I,

And by this accord, the amazement persists

At one point founded on that which I did not

Fully understand, and now augmented

By the marvels I am able to explain.

8

KEY SEOK

EVERY TIME I GO to the ocean, the scenery of the ocean makes me calm and peaceful. As you know, the vast, wide scenery makes the heart at ease. At my age, I do not really swim or go into the water; I just like to walk and watch and take a rest. That's what I usually do at the beach. I like to listen to the waves. I think most old people are like that, that is why we like the ocean.

Most Koreans usually spend their vacation on the beach during the summertime. For the wintertime, they visit the mountains instead of the beach. Seventy percent of the peninsula is mountain. Only thirty percent is flatter land. That seventy percent, however, doesn't mean that all the mountains are high like the Rocky Mountains. Some of the mountains look more like what you would call *hills* in America, so there are many trekking roads around the mountains, and most Koreans visit the mountains every weekend. That is because the room size, and the typical apartment in Korea, is very small, so people want to be out in the real world. That is why all Koreans want to be outside; the mountains are the best.

In America, Tennessee is very far from the ocean, so the driving time makes me tired, but here in Korea, the distance from Seoul to the ocean is less than an hour. Actually, Korea is at the same latitude as Tennessee, so the weather is almost the same, but the sun intensity is different, and we have the sea breeze coming in which also helps it feel cooler. Korea is a peninsula, so we have the East Sea, West Sea, and South Sea. It is easier to access the ocean on the small land (Korea) than the big land like America. The middlemost parts of the country can still easily reach the East or the West Sea. During the summertime, the East or West could be okay, but in the wintertime, we fly to Jeju Island. It is a very good place to rest, and that area is very warm all year. It's not like Hawaii, or hot like 100° F, but in the wintertime, it might be 70-80° F. In Korea, it gets hot, but not like in America. The sun is not as bright, so I get asked a lot, "How are you so tanned?" In America, I go outside for less than even an hour, and the sunlight makes me darker, but in Korea, that doesn't happen. Humidity is a very severe problem here, but the sunlight is very light compared to America. In America, I should wear sunglasses, but here in Korea, I don't need them that much.

In America, the sunlight is very bright, which makes us feel better. If you ask people who come from Iowa or Idaho, "How is your state?" They say, "Oh, beautiful, very nice!" This also happens in other states like Florida or in the South. They all say it's good and nice. That's because the sunlight is bright, so all people feel well.

I have been to Jeju Island four times in my life. I actually spent my honeymoon there. For my generation, it is more typical to go to Jeju Island for the honeymoon. Nowadays, the young people go abroad to places like Thailand or Guam, but at the time, when I was young, Jeju Island was the best honeymoon place. It was my first time to visit Jeju Island, so we visited several famous places. We went to Halla Mountain and a beach in the south of Jeju Island called Seogwipo. It's a famous place to see waterfalls and the beach and sea.

I also visited some caves. Actually, Jeju Island is volcanic, so there are some big caves there. There is one cave called Ten-Thousand-Kilometer Cave. It is not actually that big, but it seems so huge they named it like that. Inside there is water and sand, like the beach, and it is very wide and big. But now, I heard that they closed most of that because it is dangerous for people to go into because the cave has weakened, so they closed almost all of the areas. There are a few that are still open, but they were all open when I was there.

계절 (SEASONS)

No matter one's position on the globe,

the seasonality of life persists.

The warm bliss of adolescence and the brisk wisdom of age

are the same wherever I go.

여름

In my younger years, we spent our summers by the water.

The East, West, and South Seas surround Korea,

which made traveling to the balmy coastlines

an accessible option for escaping the humidity,

a stifling limitation that confined youthful energy.

I spent my honeymoon in the South Sea on Jeju Island.

It was green and flourishing, like our verdant spirits.

My bride and I soaked up our time in the sun,

investigating the many exhilarating spectacles of the isle.

Cascading waterfalls, gigantic hyperboles of caves,

and respites along the scenic beach of Seogwipo

constituted our time together.

At the time, it was typical to spend the first weeks of marriage

in this tropical paradise not far from home.

Nowadays, the young folks go abroad.

겨울

In the winter I slow down and escape to the mountains,

hill-like formations that decorate seventy percent of the land.

Trekking routes snake through these landforms, and,

as Walt Whitman once wrote,

"Afoot and light-hearted I take to the open road."

I walk,

fulfilling a thirst for the great outdoors,

trading cramped, apartment ventilation

for the crisp freshness of a winter afternoon.

The scenery lends a sense of tranquility

and makes me feel calm and at peace.

I think most old people are like that,

that is why we like the ocean.

As children, or when learning a new language, we are taught

how to say the names of different seasons throughout the year.

I teach my students learning Korean that

summer is 여름 [yeoleum] and that *winter* is 겨울 [gyeoul],

but why is it so important that we relay such knowledge?

I cannot say for sure, but I observe the patterns.

Whether in landlocked Tennessee or on the peninsula of Korea,

the seasons are the same, and I have been able to appreciate them

in new ways as I grow and walk down this path of life.

9

LESLEY

I'M NOT EXACTLY sure at this point in my life how old I was when this happened, but my dad and stepmum bought a boat. We had done a lot of sailing. My high school had a sailing team, so I had done a lot of sailing, and my dad and stepmother had done a lot of sailing. They owned a catamaran, so this was a nice, I would say, probably thirty-to-forty-foot boat, again I can't remember, but it was this old wooden boat, and it had these red and white striped sails that looked like candy, so it was pretty cool to look at.

It was me, my dad, my stepmother, and my brother who is six years younger than me. The boat was on the east coast of Scotland, and we lived on the west coast of Scotland. So, we had to go pick it up and bring it back. The easiest way to do that was to take the boat through the Crinan Canal, which separates the east coast and the west coast, and then go up the west coast to the town that we lived in, called Oban. We came through the Crinan Canal, so it was a short trip across the country instead of going up around the north because the North Sea can be pretty rough.

We went through there, and I actually haven't done the math, but I can go back and figure out what time it was because as we were coming through the canal, we stopped. There's a pub, so we all had gotten off to get some lunch, and Prince Charles and Lady Diana's wedding was showing on the television, so I specifically remember that time, but I don't remember how old I was when that happened.

We were motoring through the canal because it's not wide enough to sail, and we're going through these old loch gates because the other side of Scotland is lower than the west coast, so you have to raise the water level to get up to what it is on the other coast. When we came out of the Crinan Canal a westerly wind was coming in, and in Scotland, that's not necessarily a good thing. It comes with a lot of storms, and none of us had sailed that part of Scotland. I had only ever sailed with my high school locally, but, you know, my dad and stepmother had done a lot of orienteering and hiking and climbing and reading maps and charts because my dad was a shellfish farmer. They both were, actually. They cultivated mussels and oysters, so they had a lot of experience on the water. Although most of that experience was in a loch, they knew how to read charts, and they knew how to sail, so they were like, "No problem!"

We're heading up the west coast, and there's two islands we're passing by. One's called Scarba and the other's called Jura, and there's a very narrow gap between them which causes a lot of turbulence coming in. So... we did not time that well... and so we were coming through, and it was extremely rough. We were going through these huge waves. The Corryvrecken, they say, gets up to nine-meter waves. It was not as high as that. It was probably like four to six feet high, but it seems much higher when you're actually in the water. We were in the Dorus Mor, not in the Corryvrecken itself, which is a great feature to see. It's like a giant whirlpool, and there's lots of Scottish stories and myths about that place. Stories that they tell to make sure you don't get yourself in trouble, like those of water kelpies. They're giant, horse-like figures in Scottish lore. They've got a horse head, but obviously, they can swim underwater, so it's kind of like a mer-horse that would steal you away and take you down into the depths, and of course, you can't breathe, so that would be the end of you. Apparently, it's like the whole myth with the sirens or mermaids. They're visually enticing and beautiful, and you fall in love, and then you're like, "I'm going to be with you forever!" and then you die.

Needless to say, we're coming through there at the wrong time. My brother got really seasick, so he went down in the cabin, which was the absolute worst place to go because, at this point, we also realized that on the little boat we just bought, the engine wasn't that good, so there's like smoke all in the cabin. However, he was throwing up I think at that point, so he went down into the cabin because it was too windy to stand on the deck and throw up. The wind was coming from all the directions, so it would have just landed back on top of him, so he was doing that.

Because of the westerly gale, it is pouring down, and we can barely see like ten feet in front of us. I had gone up to the front of the boat and attached myself with a cable to the front because we couldn't see far, so I was kind of the lookout. I didn't really see that much though... At my age, I didn't really know the danger that we were in, and my dad was not really good at sharing that. So, my brother's throwing up, and I'm on the front of the boat thinking that this is the best rollercoaster in the entire world! I'm soaked, the rain is coming in from every direction, the boat is getting thrown around, and I'm like, "THIS IS THE BEST SAILING EXPERIENCE I'VE EVER HAD!" When we get through to calmer waters - there's still a gale, so it's funny to think of that as *calmer* water, but it was so much better - and I was like, "Dad! Can we do that again!" and he was like, "Absolutely not." He thought we were going to die. He *really* thought we were going to die, and I had no clue. I was just like, "THIS IS THE BEST THING IN THE ENTIRE WORLD!" Sometimes, I think naivety, and the innocence of being young, turned an ultimately really scary experience into an enjoyable one... for me anyway.

I've always had a respect for the power of the ocean and what it can do, and I've spent my entire life trying to be close to the ocean. You know, as a Scottish person I think we all feel connected to the sea; I mean, my whole life was kind of arranged around that. The water's cold, and we don't have a lot of sandy beaches, so a lot of my childhood was scrambling over rocks and finding cool stones to skim. Just the smell is something. You forget about it when you live in a different country, but as soon as you go back, you're like *this* is what I miss: the smell of the ocean and the rocks. I think in Scotland the furthest away you can get from the ocean is sixty-six miles, so I think every Scottish person has a strong connection to the ocean, but a respect too.

I grew up on the coast and did a lot of things in boats because my dad was a fish farmer, and I used to sail in high school. It's a part of everyday life. My family was lucky because that was where we lived, and even in our fun time we would go out and spend it sailing boats. I mean, our whole economy, for the most part, was tourism. People would come specifically for the food, the access to the islands, the whiskey because there's a distillery, etc. They would come to my hometown and take ferries to the islands. Oban's called the *Gateway to the Highlands and Islands*, so if you want to go anywhere on the west coast, you would have to come to my hometown.

We spent a lot of time on the islands as well because some of my high school friends lived on the islands. They would come to high school on Monday morning, stay in town, and then go back home to the islands on Friday. So, even if I went to visit a friend, there was still this connection with the sea. There's also several barrier islands in front of Oban, and so we would raise money by doing charity swims from the island to Oban. It's about a mile and a half if you include the current. One year my friends and I did it to raise money for cancer research. My dad had a boat, so we all got in the boat, and he took us over. At the time, we were contemplating if we should wear wetsuits, but it's really hard to swim in a wetsuit, so we said, "No, but let's cover our bodies in Vaseline!" Unfortunately for my dad, we did it before we went on the boat, so we were all flying all over the place, and it took him about two years to get all of the Vaseline out of the boat. It's hard to tell if it worked well or not because the water was super cold, so I don't know. It worked better than my one friend who wore the wetsuit. He had to be picked up because he couldn't move his arms enough to swim, so he didn't make it, but the rest of us did. When we stood up to get out of the water, my legs wouldn't work because they were so cold, but back then we didn't care because as kids we were like, "THIS IS THE BEST FUN EVER!" So, we spent a lot of time in the water. I mean, just everywhere is water! You've got the waterfalls, you've got the runoff, you've got the lochs, you've got the ocean itself, and the stories and the myths that were associated with that too. We were fairly close to Loch Ness, so it was always like, *if there's a Nessie, then there's got to be some sort of monster in this loch too...* It's one of those things that you know logically is not true, but when you're sitting on a boat, it's flat calm, and you can't see under the water, you just are like, *maybe there is...* The water is very ingrained into our culture.

This was definitely true with the way that we were raised. My dad being a fish farmer, we ate a lot of mussels, which doesn't sound bad, but every once and a while we would get tired of that, so we would trade mussels and oysters to get salmon. All the fishermen knew each other, and they would barter and trade different fish, and that was kind of fun too. I guess the last time my husband, Louis, and daughter, Emma, and I went was about three years ago. We went, and we hiked out, dug up some clams, and brought them back. My dad made some pasta dish with the clams, and that was kind of like our childhood too. We would just go out and forage and bring back stuff that we would find or that we would catch. Or they would hunt. I was not a fan of hunting. I shot a rabbit once. They made me gut it, and that was it, which was unfortunate because my dad would clay pigeon hunt as well, so then *I* would have to pick up the ones that people missed.

My mother worked as an accountant at what is now called the University of the Highlands and Islands, so whether I was out picking mussels with my dad, or I was at the research lab, I would hang out with the divers, and that's where I learned to dive. They would give me drysuits, and they would let me go in the bends machine. I learned all about diving from them, and I also learned how to wear a drysuit and jump off the front of a boat into the water. Because the drysuit has air, when you hit the water, you go down to a certain depth, and it will pop you back up again. It was almost as fun as going through the Corryvrecken. At one point growing up, when I was really into diving, I thought, *oooh, I'm going to be a North Sea diver!* They work for like two weeks and make enough money for almost the whole year because they're doing stuff that's super dangerous and super cold, but as I got older, I was like, *that makes no sense to me. It's too cold!*

So yeah, the water is very cold. I just have so many stories, like one time, Louis and I went back, and at the time our daughter was three or four. We were with one of my dad's friends at the pier where he had his mussel farm, and their son was like, "I'm going swimming! It's the summer!" and he jumped right in. We were like *ummm...* And Emma, who's four, is like, "I want to go in too!" so she strips down and puts one toe in there and goes "Ugh! I don't like this at all!" I used to swim in that water too, but now you would have to make me go in. To me, it feels colder than it does when we do the polar plunge here where I live now in South Carolina. The thing I also appreciated about the water in Scotland though is how clean it is. Here, I don't go swimming at the beach anymore. I used to surf, but now I don't even want to get in the water. I think it's because I know more than when I was a kid about dirty water, so I just don't get in. However, recently a friend of mine bought a sailboat, so now my favorite thing is to crew for him. We go out here, and we have to go out through the water waves of the ocean, but as soon as we turn the engine off, it all kind of comes flooding back. Except for it's incredibly hot and not like Scotland at all. Although, at my age, I kind of appreciate that. I rather be warm than sitting on a boat freezing.

As I've gotten older the charm of my hometown seems more appealing. I moved away when I was younger because Scotland is just too slow, and I think I have to do things quickly. Things are closed on Sundays, and you can't do anything because everything shuts at six o'clock. I thought, *I can't live this way; I have to go somewhere faster*, but now I'm like, *I could retire back in Scotland...* That is on the table for us at some point. We're trying to decide if we want to do that or move somewhere else in America that is more remote and more like Scotland. I guess maybe not the temperature. I'm okay if it's warmer but definitely near the water.

HOMETOWN LORE

Legends of the Corryvrecken swirl through my head

Like the whirlpool of oceanographic phenomena

That directs the mythological feat

In the channel between Scarba and Jura,

Where there await kelpies of lore,

Bent on stealing away the unsuspecting,

Lurking in the dark, numbing depths below.

I was unfamiliar with these turbulent seas,

Yet the rush invigorated my youthful spirit.

I hurried to the front of our ship and braced

Myself against the wind and crashing waves,

Drenched in rain and sticky from saltwater,

But smiling all the while.

Our little wooden boat coursed

Through the Dorus Mor under

The canopy of this vexing gale.

The red and white striped sails

Excited my childish fantasies with

Their semblance to candy as they flapped

Vigorously in the omnipresent wind.

This passage was unlike the local waters

Of my hometown, where I sailed in

High school and learned to dive and forage.

I would jump off boats into the arctic abyss,

Bobbing up to the surface again

Like a buoy in my drysuit.

We would swim there too,

But now you couldn't pay me to go in.

The biting rawness of the cold acts as a deterrent,

But back then we didn't care.

I would slip beneath the icy tundra like a fish

And flail around like one too once exposed

To the open air on the deck

Of my father's vessel,

Leaving behind traces of

Vaseline in place of scales.

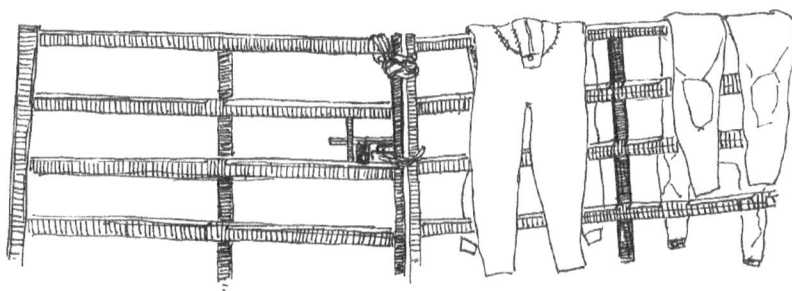

The smell of the ocean transports me

To my childhood, scrambling over rocks

And finding cool stones to skim.

It was the best fun ever.

Though a slow, fishing town,

The everyday was equipped

With unimaginable adventure,

And whether sailing through the lochs

Or exploring the waterfalls and islands,

A connection with the ocean is evident

And ingrained in the culture,

Its stories, and the people.

I was moving too fast for Oban's unhurried trod.

A charming, charismatic locale,

Where fishermen trade mussels for salmon,

And every establishment is closed on Sundays.

I had to pull away, but still, I maintain

The relationship with the sea

And spend my days chasing after it.

I once sailed

through the Crinan Canal

To get from the east coast of Scotland

To my home on the western shores.

In a similar fashion,

I now find myself

Looking from the East Coast of the United States

Back to the Highlands,

Perhaps as a refuge in retirement.

If only it weren't so cold...

10

SOPHIE

My family and I have been to a beach in Costa Rica on the Atlantic side, so that's the most beautiful beach or part of the ocean that I've ever been to. We go there because our family friends have a hotel there that they run. They used to live in Nashville and then just up and moved to Costa Rica one day, so they decided to open a really beautiful hotel there. We usually get the friend discount. The hotel is gorgeous; they call it Tiki Lodge. Everything in Costa Rica is just centered around the nature, and the hotel itself is really just rooms facing the outdoors. They're kind of peppered around this beautiful green area that's really well-kept with lots of palm trees, and then there's a pool in the middle of the grounds area, so the little peppered rooms surround it. Then there is the main office, which is next to the pool, and then above the main office was the treetop house, which is the room that we would rent. It was their best room, and it's almost like a treehouse because there are trees just everywhere. It was this entire house eye-level with all the tops of the trees. It had two bedrooms and a loft, and then it had the most beautiful patio surrounding the entire house. There was just all this sitting area with lots of wonderful hammocks that you could sit in all the time, and they had beautiful couches, and you could see a lot of the trees and the surrounding mountains. Costa Rica's got some beautiful big hills.

We usually spend two or three days just lounging around on the beach. We have all these plans for when we get there, and then we just spend a week at the beach because we are so lazy, and the beach just takes over our entire selves, but it's always so wonderful. It always feels like such a refreshing trip. We've been a total of three times in my life; each time has been different and so beautiful. I think my parents are trying to make it a normal place for us to retreat to.

The hotel's really nice because they give yoga classes every morning. I remember the yoga instructor was like SUPER pregnant when she was giving her class, but she was still so skinny and doing the craziest yoga all with this little baby in her stomach. It was really something. We went back a different time, and she had had the baby, and the baby would sit around while they were doing yoga classes. It was really cute! I love that progression of time.

Sometimes I'll take surfing lessons. I've taken a couple surfing lessons throughout my life, and it's been incredible! I've been standing up on the board for about half a second out of my entire life, and it's something that I remember so vividly in my head. I love it so much! If I had more guts, I would surf more, but I just get stressed about the back of the board hitting my head when I go under and then thinking I'd just die. I'm scared because when I was doing surfing lessons, they said to make sure when you go down you cover your head because the little fin on the bottom of the board is really sharp. If you're going under the board, for whatever reason, and the tide picks up the board, it could smack you with it... It's actually nerve-wracking. Yeah, this is probably not the most calming and wonderful story about the ocean, but a lot of it is scary, and a lot about surfing is scary. The tide rolls, and so you can get flipped over and flipped over and not stop, and it can break your board in half if you're not careful because the tide is so powerful! Oh my gosh, it's so powerful, and the beach that we go to is considered a very gentle beach! Boogie boarding is actually my personal favorite because it's all the fun and none of the stress. You can still go pretty hard on a boogie board!

I've been dolphin-watching on a boat when we've also been able to get off the boat and swim in the water and look at the coastal coral reefs. It's beautiful! I've seen so many beautiful fish swimming around the reefs just from looking up above to down below. It's awesome! You can see everything all the way down to the bottom. It's so clear and wonderful! That's probably my favorite memory from Costa Rica, but also, when I was maybe seven or eight – this is probably controversial now for good reasons, but when I was like seven it was totally okay – we went out to the beach at night and had a tour guide show us sea turtles that came to shore and were laying their eggs. It was insane! They were in that comatose state where they are perched over the holes that they dug and laying their eggs. While they were in that comatose state, we were able to (much to my chagrin in hindsight) shine flashlights and watch as the eggs left their bodies and fell to the ground. It was insane and so cool! They are so big! They are beautiful and old and so cool!

I love the monkeys, too! They're like squirrels down there! They're cute monkeys, and when I was there last time, they had babies! It was really precious and so cute! I love them. They would balance on telephone wires the way that squirrels do and were just walking across them.

My favorite memory of going to the beach, well aside from the turtles (that was really cool!), and aside from the corals (that was really cool too!), was when I was really young and we went horseback riding on the beach, which is my favorite thing to do. It was just as the sun was rising in the morning. We were riding these beautiful, little horses, and then a big gust of wind swept through, and I was wearing a little pink hat, and it took my hat right off and sent it into the sea, never to be seen again. It was such a beautiful day, and then I lost a hat... but it was okay. I was just so tickled by how beautiful everything was that I didn't mind. I mean, I got a really bad sunburn after, but other than that...

ISLAND IN THE TREES

Under the serenity of closed eyes,

I picture an island in my mind,

Where the qualities of everyday life

Defy the ordinary.

There is an abode in the sky,

And now I am sleeping in the treetops,

Where nature wraps her arms around me

In a warm embrace,

Encompassing every aspect of my existence.

I am neighbors with the monkeys,

And the dolphins say hello.

The hills undulate beyond the veranda

Like the rhythm of the waves in the ocean.

Movement and energy exude from every corner,

And upon arriving at this lofty oasis,

The beach takes over my entire self.

I get lost in its intensity, which terrifies

And amazes me in the same breath.

In one instant it has the strength

To rip me away from secure footing

And toss me relentlessly

In a foamy, unfamiliar realm.

But still, I surf,

And in the half a second of my life

Where the board, the waves,

And I seem to get along,

I am on top of the world.

Water, however, is a polar molecule.

Although on one hand, it strikes me

With the fear of impending danger,

At another juncture it is gentle

And takes me down

Enticing, coralline routes

That lead to

Colorful, aquatic cities

Of vivacious splendor.

Legend has it that

At a certain time of year

Reptilian giants emerge

Under the ebon veil

Of the island night sky.

I sneak away in the quiet of the evening

To see if the myth holds true.

I catch glimpse of the rumored beings

And am taken aback by the girth

Of the creature before me.

I watch closely as she buries a treasure

Of the finest pearls

Under the lithogeny of the coast

Before slipping away to the

Inky waters from whence she came.

These reveries of recollection fill me

With fantastical enthusiasm,

And on horseback, I ride across

The dreamy shoreline such happy musings

Create within the psyche.

I feel the wind rush through my hair,

And I lose a part of myself to the sea

While the joy of being alive prompts me forward

Towards the rising sun

That invites a new day.

11

MEG & AARON

MEG

I'm trying to think of the first time I ever saw an ocean... I must've been a kid. Nothing memorable there. I think in general I just like water and love to be in water. Like, if we are at a pool, just swimming, I'm the first one in, last one out. I grew up in Colorado, so we didn't have any oceans, but I had family in California. I think it took me awhile to understand that not all parts of California are warm all year round, so a lot of my first experiences with the ocean were just cold. It was just not what I was seeing in movies or TV shows. I think the first time I felt real, warm ocean water was probably when Aaron and I went to the Gulf. That trip is where this new obsession with water kind of started, or I guess more of continued, with me.

AARON

My mom grew up in Charleston, South Carolina, and my dad met her down there, and he brought her back to Sparta, Tennessee, which is where I grew up. When I was a kid, we would go back every year to visit her family who were still in Charleston, and we always went to the beach while we were there, so there was always a beach trip. Sometimes the jellyfish were out, and we didn't get to go in the water. Sometimes we didn't know the jellyfish were out, and we went in the water anyway and got stung.

So yeah, it was fun. I only got scared one time because we were swimming around, and something swam up against my arm. I don't know what it was. At the time I thought it was an octopus, but an octopus wouldn't feel like that, so it was probably just a fish. Or maybe it was just my sister swimming next to me, and she kicked my arm, but it scared me.

One year we were there, and we were swimming, and my sister started screaming, and we all got worried because we didn't know what had happened to her. We got her out of the ocean, and she lifted her foot up, and there was a little crab. He wasn't pinching her, but his shell was so sharp it stuck into the side of her toe. She's definitely not a person who likes crawly things. She freaks out at just the word spider, and she is kind of squeamish, so that makes sense that she freaked out as a child.

✺✺✺

The first time we went to the Gulf down in Destin was for our one-year anniversary, and we tried to do as many things as we could. We went parasailing, and we took a sunset dolphin cruise about an hour outside up the bank. I had only been living in Nashville for a year, and I met him two weeks after I moved here. I mean, I've been here ten years now, but when I first moved here, throughout our whole first year of dating, we went and did a bunch of stuff. We've been road tripping, and we travel all over the place. Growing up in Colorado, it's such a big state, it would take forever just to get to another state, but here in Tennessee, you drive just seven hours from Nashville and you're on the coast in Florida. A seven-hour drive in Colorado, you're still in Colorado.

So, to celebrate our first anniversary, we went to Destin, and we got a condo on the beach with a balcony that faced the ocean. We kept the balcony doors open the whole four days we were there. We had some wine and would just sit and read in the living room for hours and then would go and sit on the beach and read for a couple hours. He would like play in the sand or build sandcastles and then play in the water. I love water so much, and it was like, oh my gosh, this soothes my soul inside! I have this huge, warm bathwater pool-thing that I get to look forward to playing in! That was a good end to my first year being on this side of the country. I have this whole other world open to me where it's very realistic to get to an ocean, and it's a different kind of ocean than what I was used to growing up with. I got to see that, oh my gosh, the ocean, it's warm! And it's like a teal-greenish color rather than this dark, scary, black-blue color! The sand was really, really soft, and there's so many people out playing and doing all these things, like parasailing! I never had that option growing up visiting family on the West Coast. It was kind of weird, not like a social shock to the system, but different nonetheless, and it all kind of got tagged onto all the newness of that first year of living on this side of the country.

I'm a huge adrenaline junkie too, so I love any of that jumping-off things, skydiving, parasailing type deal, so I dragged him along to do that kind of stuff. Parasailing is one of the few things that we hadn't forced him to do yet, so that was one of the things that we did during that trip. He didn't like it because – I mean, he also doesn't like heights – a week before we even left for that trip and were thinking of doing it, some malfunction happened on another parasailing thing. The cord cut, and the people went flying.

No, that's not what happened. The harness broke, and the girl fell down and died.

I thought you said that the thing broke and then flew into the side of a cliff?

No.

That's what I remember you telling me. Falling two hundred feet into the ocean, if you fell right, you wouldn't have died.

You could die.

Yeah, but she probably didn't fall right. I remember you telling me very different because you didn't want the thing to break and for us to like fly away.

It would have been fine. We would have just floated down.

No... Anyways, so I convinced him to do it, and we did it, and it was so much fun! I would totally do it again! I don't know about him though...

I would do it again; I would just be scared again.

He does a lot of things scared, and I force him to do it. We've gone skydiving three times, and we've gone hang gliding. He hasn't bungee jumped, and he hasn't done the high cliff diving, so parasailing is probably pretty up there for his adrenaline.

That's probably the only thing that really stands out to me ocean-wise. I very much like the Gulf, and we've joked that whenever we can retire sometime, we'll for sure get a condo on the beach, basically just based on how relaxed we were on that one trip.

Getting to associate with beach trips has been so fun now, especially getting to be with his family too. It's been fun to be a part of his family because his dad's side, here in Sparta, is a big family, and then his mom's side of the family is actually still in Charleston, so we had a huge family-get-together back in June of 2021. We rented this huge beach house and were right across the street from the beach, and we got to hang out with his cousins and aunts and uncles and his mom's cousins.

People were coming from Kansas City, and California, and all over the place.

Yeah, people came from all over just to like hang out for this week. It was a huge family reunion. He was meeting people, and he was like, "We're related, good to meet you! I've never known about you," "What cousin are you?" or "Who are you with?"

They would pull out a picture like, "Hey, here's all of you together!"

and I was like, "I don't know."

Getting to do this reunion was also kind of like, oh my gosh, you're a part of this huge family! I was surprised, even in preparing for the trip and getting in contact with all the family members, everyone was all definitely like, "Yeah! I'm gung-ho!" and "Count me in! Let's do the beach house reunion!" After the fact, they even talked about how fun it was and how we should do it again.

The chunks of us had our own beach house, so we were with his sister, her kids, his parents, and then his cousin and his wife who live in Charleston. They were like, "We won't commute every day to come see you. We'll take the week, and we'll come and stay with you guys, and we'll get a big beach house." They go out in the ocean and all that stuff all the time, so they were definitely pros when it came to, "Okay guys, let's pack up and walk across the street and set up the tents..." and, you know, whatever. They had all the toys.

Yeah, they came prepared with a tent and a cooler for beer.

And this umbrella-machine-kind-of-thing that you stick in the ground and drill into the sand deep down, so then you can put your umbrella on the beach. They had so many things! And I got super, super sunburnt on my back because I didn't know that the sand reflects up and like sunburns you.

And the water reflects.

Noooo!

Aaron and his sister would talk about his past childhood Charleston trips. She's got three kids, so getting to take them over the years for their first times and their first trips to Charleston was a lot of fun. For us, this trip was super fun because we got to take our dog, Bert, and see how she reacted to the ocean and the sand, and how she really liked it.

She was kind of iffy about the waves coming up.

The small waves were about twice as big as she was.

But if we were both standing in the water, she would try to come to us. So, she would swim around a little, but she definitely liked running up and down the beach the best. She loved running in that sand. She would dig her little head and dig holes and stuff. She very much really loved being at the beach!

Yep.

Which was good, because I wouldn't have wanted her to have a weird experience, and then we could never take her again in the future.

That first day it was really windy, and the sand was blasting her,

so we had to pick her up and carry her.

We're kind of obsessed with her...

DESTINATION

MEG

I grew up in a landlocked state,
But I had family who lived on the
West Coast.

And as a kid,
I stared into the cold, black waters
Of the California shore.

Not many ocean memories stand out
From my childhood,

But when I moved to the
Other side of the country,
I met Aaron, and
We took a trip to Destin
After that first year together.

We stayed in a condo by the water
And opened every door to the outside
So as to welcome in the freshness
Of this paradise on the Gulf,
Letting the summery air envelop
The space and fill the atmosphere.

I got to experience a whole different world,
Where the ocean is a sparkling,
Teal-green pool of foamy bathwater,

AARON

I grew up in a landlocked state,
But I had family who lived on the
East Coast.

And as a kid,
I played with my sister on the warm, sandy
Shores of South Carolina.

I have lots of stories
From our annual, family beach trips.

My parents met in Charleston, and
I grew up in Sparta, Tennessee.
Later, I met Meg, and
We took a trip to Destin
After that first year together.

We stayed in a condo by the water
And opened every door to the outside
So as to welcome in the freshness
Of this paradise on the Gulf,
Letting the summery air envelop
The space and fill the atmosphere.

I got to return to my childhood,
Where the beach is one large sandbox
Brimming with creative potential,

Radiating and immaculate

In the most astounding aquamarine hues.

I got burnt because I did not know the sun

Reflected off the sand and sea.

We did all kinds of things.

I'm kind of an adrenaline junkie, so

We went parasailing...

It was awesome.

The clock seemed to stand still,

But hours went by without notice.

We would read in the infinity of these

Moments, ignorant of the passage of time.

Throughout the duration of my dwelling

On this side of the country,

I have gotten the opportunity to

Appreciate such luxurious excursions,

Not only as relaxing getaways,

But also as delightful roads

That bring individuals together.

I love getting to associate

With this type of beach trip,

Inviting me to build sandcastles

From piles of sediment upon the oceanfront.

I soaked up the familiar warmth of the sun

Reflected off the sand and sea.

We did all kinds of things.

I'm not much of a thrill-seeker, but

We went parasailing...

It was terrifying.

The clock seemed to stand still,

But hours went by without notice.

We would read in the infinity of these

Moments, ignorant of the passage of time.

In our old age, I hope we retire

To the Gulf, primarily based on how

Relaxing that blissful sojourn was,

But for the time being, the continued

Family vacations to Charleston

More than suffice as welcome reprieves

From the humdrum of the everyday.

This coastal city where my mother grew up,

A haven of my youth, in which

This new perspective
Of family vacation.

My sister and I were sheltered
Across many summers.

It is rewarding to now get to spend these
Intermissions as a married couple
And watch our nieces and nephews
And beloved dog, Bert, discover
The ocean for the first time.

It is rewarding to now get to spend these
Intermissions as a married couple
And watch our nieces and nephews
And beloved dog, Bert, discover
The ocean for the first time.

I suppose as a child it had a similar purpose.
I was swept away from the life I knew
In the landlocked purgatory
Of Colorado to spend a stint of time
On the seashores of California, visiting family,
Coming together because of the sea, but it all
Looks so different from this new lens.

I am glad we have been able to relish
In the goodness of this place
Over many generations.
Even as my family expands to include
New members and different personalities,
The dependability of this maternal locale
Roots me in stories of my past.

Now I get to watch Bert explore this world
In her own way: digging holes in the sand
And running along the shore.
She's scared of the water, like we were as kids,
But embraces the novelty of it all
With wide, puppy-dog eyes.

Now I get to watch Bert explore this world
In her own way: digging holes in the sand
And running along the shore.
She's scared of the water, like we were as kids,
But embraces the novelty of it all
With wide, puppy-dog eyes.

Oh, Bert.
We're kind of obsessed with her...

Oh, Bert.
We're kind of obsessed with her...

POSTSCRIPT

WHEN ORIGINALLY PLANNING out this collection of pieces, I was not expecting to add my own story to the script. After discussing the organization of the final product with my advisor, we decided it would be appropriate to include a postscript dictating my own run-in with the sea. Hesitant, yet agreeable nonetheless, this is me attempting to fulfill that component of the project; however, upon consenting to partake in such an endeavor, I ran into the same dilemma that I knowingly put each of my participants through: figuring out which story to tell. Having faced this semi-existential conundrum, I am now ready to write my tale.

Let me take you to the rolling hills of the Scottish Highlands in the small, coastal town of Oban. It is here that I spent a brief spell to study oceanography through an opportunity offered at my university in conjunction with the Scottish Association for Marine Science (SAMS). My group arrived at the beginning of May just after the spring semester had ended. The hillsides were hemmed with bluebells, and Welsh poppies grew in every nook and cranny of the land. The institution itself was right on the water, and on breaks we would explore the area around it, scaling the cliffs that edged the sea. The ground atop the hills was plush, as years of grassy die off and regrowth layered the earth. I was both terrified and intrigued to think about what sort of things were hidden within, buried under years of wild vegetation. The charcoal-gray rocks along the cliff faces that turned toward the open sea were stippled with constellations of different colored lichen. They came in crusty, white patches; foliated clusters of pastel green; deltas of reddish-purple; seafoam, grass-like shoots; and, my personal favorite, dabs of bright orange! Alongside the glorious lichens were an array of mosses and coastal flora such as thrift, *Armenia maritima*, which kind of reminds me of the flowers in *Horton Hears a Who.*

Beyond the window of the room where we ate our lunches at the school, I saw an oystercatcher for the first time. For those who may be unfamiliar with this specimen, it is a splendid bird clad in black and white with the most stunning orange beak! It gracefully swoops and dives into the sea in a flash of all these colors to catch its meals. I was pleased we could dine together in this way.

In stark contrast to the delightful oystercatcher, there was one annoying seagull that would pester my friends and me for French fries. Sometimes for dinner, we would walk to the local fish and chips shop for take-away. The fish was always fresh haddock, and the cooks would douse the chips with salt and vinegar if you so chose (which you always should!). The tantalizing meal was packed in a cardboard box that was about the same height as a typical pizza box, but rectangular and much smaller. We would then eat beside the water or on one of the benches looking out to the sea. This is where I met my new frenemy, the gull. I am convinced he was the same one every time. There was an evil look in his eye, and he had this stance about him like he was bent on thievery.

The gull was but a minor disturbance in the grand scheme of things. In fact, sometimes I rather sympathized with him. In the end, however, no matter where this particular seagull landed on the evil scale, there was so much more goodness to behold in this beautiful place. One aspect that stands out in my recollections is the vivid color pallet of Scotland. It brings to mind the vibrant, wild fuschia plants I saw on my walks in Oban. The fuschia was an exceptionally exciting find because I had written a paper about it for a class. Now I got to see the mystical botanic grow wild in person. Once on a walk with a friend on a road parallel to the shore, we came across a fuschia bush with several happy little bumblebees. To our surprise, and utter delight, we noticed that the bees had white bums. With this new detail in mind, I began to see these white-bummed bumbles everywhere. I would later learn that they are called whitetail bumblebees, *Bombus lucorum.*

My absolute favorite color is orange. I am not quite sure exactly why, but something about it deeply pleases me, and it has always been my preferred hue. A friend of mine relayed a conversation he once had with another individual. They were talking about favorite colors, and this individual expressed that her favorite color was pink. She then proceeded to explain that she liked pink because every time you see it in nature, it is absolutely stunning. For me, the color orange has a similar appeal. In our spare time in Scotland, either within the protected bays near SAMS or in the town of Oban itself, I liked to walk along the exposed rocky coastline and cobbled beaches at low tide. On my first day there I noticed a little orange snail shell. It was Cheeto-like in color and reminded my friends and me of macaroni. From then on, when I wandered the shore, I would collect these empty, orange shells in my pocket, along with bits of sea glass, and the occasional cool rock. By the end of the trip, I had a whole stash.

It is also on these wandering expeditions that I found my favorite macroalgae, the best thing that I never knew existed until then. It was a type of *Enteromorpha,* fluorescent green in color and growing in crinkly strands. The membranous tissue was translucent and trapped within each tubular strand were bubbles of air. It reminded me of mermaids' hair, and the first time I saw it, I knew I had to touch it! Few things are as incredible as squatting in your rainboots over a pool of tepid seawater on a rocky, Scottish beach and playing with the radioactive-looking tendrils from large clumps of *Enteromorpha spp.* seaweed.

The sediments along the beaches and inlets were cobbles. Some were flat and smooth, so I learned to skip rocks here. For me personally, this was a particularly grand accomplishment, for I did not have this skill beforehand, but often yearned to wield it. Every morning we would wait for the bus provided through the public transit system. Never really being one to sit and wait, I would use this time to mosey around the shoreline closest to the bus stop. Sometimes I would practice my rock-skipping, other times I would just stand on one of the boat ramps and stare down into the sea. In the mornings, you see, the tide was rather high, so all the rocks, seaweed, and other features that I usually saw exposed on the shore were in their underwater element. The seaweed, a type of *Fucus* I believe, would sway with the waves' ebb and flow. Their airy gas bladders (pneumatocysts) kept them afloat, making the aquatic photosynthesizers look alive, rather than limp along the beach. It was during such observations that I met my fisherman friend. One morning, while I was gazing at the new realm of high tide, a boat pulled up alongside the ramp. An older man with white wispy hair and a lovely smile exited the boat with a bucket in tow. He wore yellow rain boots (or wellies as those in the UK would say). I don't know when we started chatting, but I do know that I made a lovely new friend that day. He told me he went out every morning. His life was molded by the local waters, and the ocean was integrated into his everyday. Growing up in the landlocked state of Tennessee, this was quite an interesting contrast to comprehend. We both loved the sea, but it was a key feature in our respective lives for very different reasons. For me, being by the water is an occasion, whereas for him, it was a living. That was the first and last time that I came across this benevolent stranger, but he left a lasting impression, and the memory of our encounter is one that I continue to cherish.

HIGHLAND HUES

During my time away, folded in the plush hills

Of a tucked-away corner of the Earth,

I put on a pair of rose-colored glasses

Through which I was able to better see

The dazzling tones of the great Scottish Highlands.

The vibrant magenta and deep purple hues of wild fuschia,

And the bumblebees with their white rumps

Buzzing along buttery yellow Welsh poppies,

The same shade as my new friend's wellies,

Instilled in me something extraordinarily dear

That I continue to cherish.

Bluebells dotted the hillsides that I drove past

On shuttle trips to and from class.

From the window of the lunchroom,

I saw an oystercatcher,

A pure blur of orange, black, and white,

Dive into the deep azure sea, edged in dark cliffs.

The geology of this exposed terrain was painted

With the varying chromatics of splotchy lichen

In an array of violet-tinted red, white, pastel green,

And, my personal favorite, orange patches.

There is something so splendid about the color orange;

Such was the color of the little shells I collected

Along the shores of Oban, in between trifling about

With the fluorescent green tangle of mermaids' hair

Revealed to me in the tepid pools

Abandoned about the rocky coast.

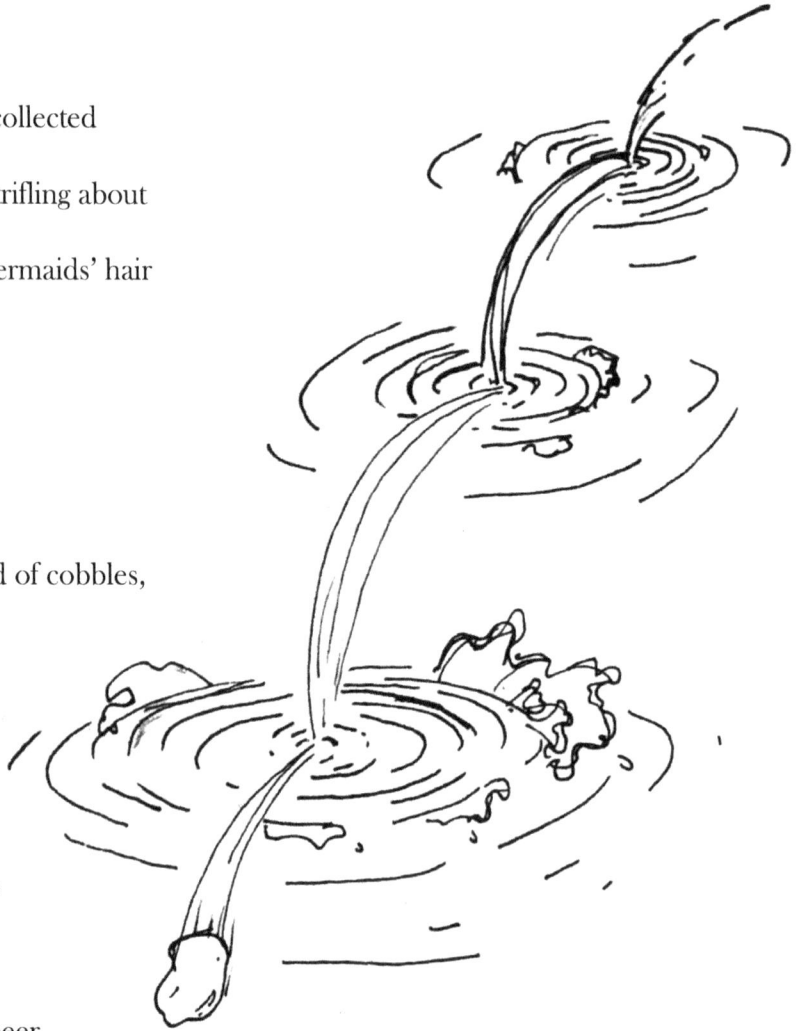

The inlets and beaches were comprised of cobbles,

And within these enclaves I procured

The delicate art of rock-skipping.

I would practice my new skill

While waiting for the red morning bus,

Otherwise using this precious time to peer

Over the boat ramp at the lively underwater realm below.

Galaxies of snails upon the concrete siding

And swaying cities of seaweed at high tide

Composed the mental images that I captured

During these brief endeavors.

On longer expeditions, adorned in my blue rainboots,

I moseyed around the coastline in awe

Of the color, life, and structures surrounding me.

I collected bits of this place as I went,

But I think I left a part of myself as well.

Planted in the deep layers of biotic carpet

That fabricate the topography,

Billowing greenery, thick from years of rebirth,

And trusty confidant to the weathered secrets within.

Rounded shards of sea glass, shelly debris,

And intriguing fragments of rock

Amassed in the secure confines of my pockets,

While I relinquished iotas of my soul

To be scattered about the land I trod.

Strewn like magic,

A fairy dust that would bring us together again,

The colors of Scotland

And I.

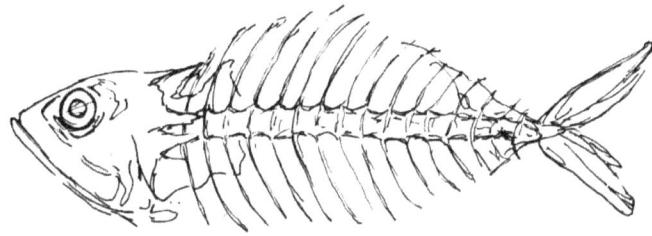

Fin

A NOTE FROM THE AUTHOR

LOOKING BACK, I am very proud of what I was able to accomplish as the capstone to my academic career thus far. The pure joy of imagination and creativity involved helped lift my spirits in a trying time, and through conversations with the participants I was able to surround myself with community. For me this process reiterated the goal of the project itself: we are all connected through the ocean. Nature is a creative force that can open our eyes to a world of possibility and connection, so thank you to anyone who has decided to partake in this literary journey. Completing this project was definitely one of the more frustrating experiences I have endured. The collection was written during a difficult time with the many uncertainties and challenges involved with a worldwide pandemic. I, myself, was also going through a difficult spell and feeling quite sad and lonely. The age of COVID-19 really did a number on my undergraduate plans, but through these obstacles I was able to think, problem-solve, and interact with people and my degree in a way that I would not have been able to before. Despite the hair-splitting saga of aggravation that it took to finalize the product, the actual act of creating these poems and illustrations was some of my most exciting and meaningful work. I hope the pieces were able to bring you some sense of peace. You are never alone.